Minuteman Missile Sites
Management Alternatives
Environmental Assessment

Department of the Interior
National Park Service

Department of Defense
US Air Force
Legacy Resource Management Program

The Minuteman Missile

The images of the Cold War are etched in our national memory — Sputnik, the Berlin Wall, bomb shelters, duck-and-cover drills, the arms race, peaceniks, and Peacekeepers.

Some of the most vivid images are of the Cuban Missile Crisis of 1962, when the United States and the Soviet Union came closer to nuclear war than at any time in history. As the world watched, Soviet leader Nikita Khrushchev and President John F. Kennedy engaged in a showdown over US demands that the Soviet Union remove its missiles from Cuba. It was at this moment, the most dangerous in the Cold War, that the Minuteman intercontinental ballistic missile (ICBM) came on line. President Kennedy later called it his *ace in the hole*.

One of the most significant strategic weapons in history, the Minuteman was America's first push-button — literally *turn-key* — nuclear missile. This marriage of rocketry and nuclear power created a weapon for which there was virtually no defense. Once the launch command was given and the keys were turned, a Minuteman missile could deliver its thermonuclear warhead to a Soviet target within a half hour.

Now, changes in the world situation have created an opportunity to preserve a historic Minuteman missile complex — Ellsworth Air Force Base's Delta One and Delta Nine — which could provide future generations a close-up view of one of America's most important Cold War weapons.

FRONT COVER PHOTOGRAPH
A Minuteman I ICBM launches during a test flight at Cape Canaveral, Florida, in 1961. US AIR FORCE

BACK COVER PHOTOGRAPH
Artwork on Delta One LCC blast door. SAYRE HUTCHISON

PAGE TWO PHOTOGRAPHS & GRAPHICS
When launched from an underground silo, a distinctive white smoke ring accompanied the Minuteman launch. US AIR FORCE

Nuclear test explosion. SMITHSONIAN INSTITUTION

Sputnik newspaper headline, 1957. WESTERN HISTORY DEPARTMENT, DENVER PUBLIC LIBRARY

Family bomb shelter, 1955. UPI PHOTOGRAPH ENTITLED, "H-BOMB HIDEAWAY" IN GARDEN CITY, NEW YORK, 1955

PAGE THREE PHOTOGRAPHS & GRAPHICS
A Launch Control Center crew on duty in Delta One. ROBERT LYON

President John F. Kennedy. WESTERN HISTORY DEPARTMENT, DENVER PUBLIC LIBRARY

Protesters. AP/WIDE WORLD PHOTOS

Lunar lander. RICHARD M. KOHEN

President George Bush & Soviet leader Mikhail Gorbachev sign START Treaty. AP/WIDE WORLD PHOTOS

Delta Nine missile extraction. SAYRE HUTCHISON

PHOTOGRAPH AT RIGHT
A Minuteman team prepares a Delta Flight missile for removal. SAYRE HUTCHISON

1995, Denver: National Park Service, Rocky Mountain Region.

First Edition

Printing 9 8 7 6 5 4 3 2 1

PUBLICATION DESIGN BY RICHARD M. KOHEN

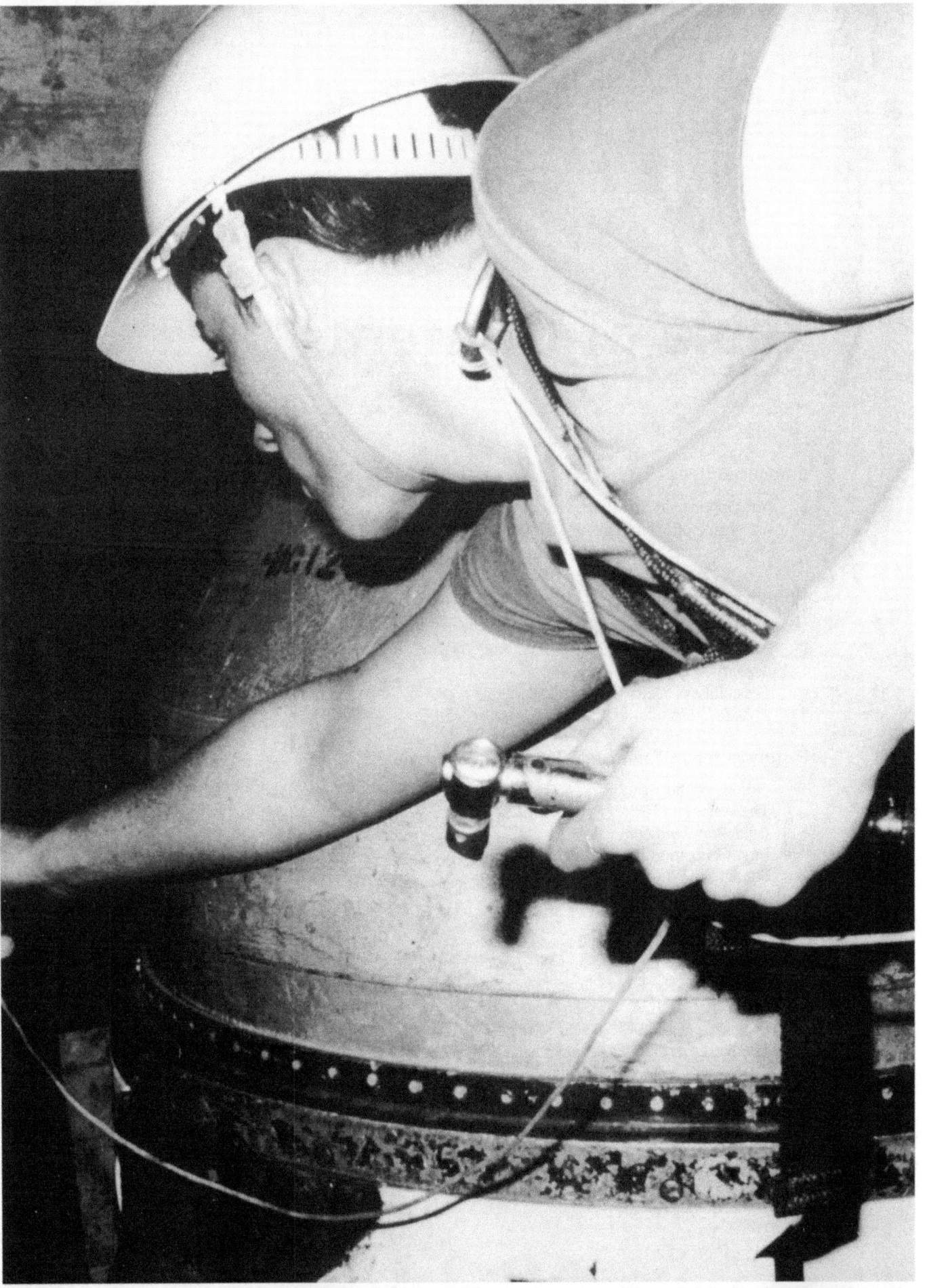

Table of Contents

Introduction 9

    An Opportunity for Preservation / 10
    Summary of Management Alternatives / 10
    Visitor Center Alternatives / 11

Criteria for Parklands 13

    National Significance of Delta One and Delta Nine / 13
    Suitability of Delta One and Delta Nine / 16
    Vicinity Map / 17
    Feasibility of Delta One and Delta Nine / 18
    President Eisenhower's Farewell Address / 19

History of the Minuteman ICBM Missile System 21

    Origins of the Arms Race / 22
    The American ICBM Program / 23
    Cold War Time Line / 24
    First Generation ICBMs: Atlas and Titan / 26
    Strength in Numbers: The Missile Gap / 28
    Weapon System "Q" / 29
    Minuteman I / 30
    The "Underground" Air Force / 32
    Minuteman Deployment and Site Selection / 33
    Minuteman Comes to Ellsworth Air Force Base / 33
    A Silo A Day / 34
    Backbone of the US Nuclear Arsenal / 36
    The Next Generations: Minuteman II and III / 39
    Deactivation of the Minuteman II Weapon System / 42

Site Description 45

    Delta One / 45
    Delta Nine / 54

Description of Management Alternatives 59

    Common Elements / **59**
    Alternative 1 / **60**
    Alternative 2 / **61**
    Alternative 3 / **62**
    Other Alternatives Considered / **67**

Possible Visitor Center Locations 69

    Exit 131 / **69**
    Badlands National Park / **69**
    Exit 127 / **69**
    Exit 121 / **69**
    Exit 116 / **71**
    Exit 110 / **71**
    South Dakota Air and Space Museum / **71**
    Pros and Cons of Visitor Center Type and Location / **72**

Environmental Assessment 77

    Viewshed Analysis / **77**
    Topography / **77**
    Climate and Weather / **77**
    Soils / **78**
    Vegetation / **78**
    Wildlife / **79**
    Endangered, Threatened, or Candidate Species / **79**
    Flood Plains / **79**
    Wetlands / **80**
    Hazardous Materials / **80**

Socioeconomic Analysis 83

    Regional Overview / **83**
    The Vacation Travel Industry / **84**
    Vacation Travel Spending / **86**
    Vehicular Traffic Patterns / **86**
    Visitation Potential at Minuteman Missile National Historic Site / **87**
    Exit 131 Visitor Center Estimates / **88**

Summary of Public Responses 91

    Public Participation Process / **93**
    Public Support for the Management Alternatives / **93**
    Minuteman Missile National Historic Site Visitor Center:
        A Stand-Alone or Multi-Resource Center? / **94**
    Preferred Location of the Visitor Center / **96**

Bibliography 99

Study Team Members 103

Introduction

In 1961, the US Air Force began constructing 1,000 Minuteman ICBM missile sites in America's heartland. Dispersed in underground silos throughout the central United States, Minuteman missiles were inconspicuous, silent sentinels on the Nation's rural landscape. Casual observers, including the thousands of tourists who annually traveled along Interstate 90 in western South Dakota, could easily have overlooked the antennas and security fencing that were the only "topside" signs of the below-ground, nuclear-tipped missiles.

The Minuteman missile system's carefully-designed, low-profile appearance only underscored its top-secret importance to national security. For almost 30 years, Minuteman missiles served as an integral component of America's nuclear triad of land-based ICBMs, submarine-launched missiles, and manned bombers. Although never launched against an enemy target, the Minuteman weapon system's ability to unleash apocalyptic destructive power at a moment's notice made "hot war" unthinkable — and protracted the standoff of the Cold War.

But by 1989, it was clear that the nearly 45-year-long Cold War between the world's superpowers was coming to a close. The Berlin Wall crumbled, Germany reunified, and former Eastern Bloc nations replaced their Communist regimes with democratically-elected governments. As a new decade and new world order began, the Soviet Union disintegrated. In 1991, when the Warsaw Pact dissolved, the enemy that President Ronald Reagan had once called "the evil empire" ceased to exist.

The Strategic Arms Reduction Treaty (START), which US President George Bush and Soviet leader Mikhail Gorbachev signed in Moscow on July 31, 1991, reflected these changes in the world situation. As part of that effort to reduce the number of ICBMs worldwide, the Air Force began deactivating the Nation's entire Minuteman II force. Among the Minuteman sites to be deactivated were the 150 missile silos and 15 launch control facilities of the 44th Missile Wing at Ellsworth Air Force Base (AFB) in South Dakota.

Left: *A Minuteman I missile test launch at Vandenberg Air Force Base in California, August 1973. The Minuteman intercontinental ballistic missile (ICBM) could reach targets a continent away. The missiles traveled out of the atmosphere and returned to earth at tremendous velocities, upwards of 15,000 miles per hour. "Ballistic" missiles are so named because, after a short period of powered flight, they assume a ballistic path, acted on only by gravity and, during reentry, by the friction of the atmosphere.* US AIR FORCE

After signing the START Treaty in Moscow on July 31, 1991, President George Bush and Soviet leader Mikhail Gorbachev exchange pens, which were made from the remnants of destroyed missiles.

AN OPPORTUNITY FOR PRESERVATION

Soon after the deactivation began, the National Park Service and the Air Force recognized that Ellsworth AFB's Minuteman facilities might be excellent candidates for long-term preservation. The Ellsworth AFB sites are among the Nation's oldest Minuteman missile bases. They are also the least altered from the original Minuteman configuration, much of their technology dating to the era of the Cuban Missile Crisis.

Thus, the end of the Cold War created a unique "window of opportunity" to preserve a historic Minuteman missile complex. Through an interagency agreement, the National Park Service and the Air Force agreed to temporarily preserve two representative Minuteman sites at Ellsworth AFB — the Delta One Launch Control Facility and the Delta Nine Launch Facility — until their long-term preservation could be evaluated.

In December 1993, the National Park Service began a special resource study of Delta One and Delta Nine. The Minuteman Special Resource Study Team — which included representatives from the National Park Service, the US Air Force, the US Air Force Museum, the South Dakota Historical Society, and the Ellsworth Heritage Foundation — spent much of the past year evaluating the possible preservation of Delta One and Delta Nine and making them available to the public as historic sites. Presented here are the findings of that study.

SUMMARY OF MANAGEMENT ALTERNATIVES

The Minuteman Special Resource Study Team developed three management alternatives for the historic missile facilities at Ellsworth AFB:

Under **Alternative 1**, no action would be taken and Delta One and Delta Nine would not be preserved. The Air Force would deactivate and demolish Delta One and Delta Nine, as is currently underway with all of the other Minuteman sites associated with the 44th Missile

Wing. This alternative received little support from the public.

Under **Alternative 2**, a government agency or non-profit organization — *but not the National Park Service* — would acquire Delta One and Delta Nine and make them available for public visitation. Despite widespread publicity about the Minuteman Special Resource Study, no government agency or non-profit organization has come forward and expressed a willingness to take over Delta One and Delta Nine. This alternative also received little support from the public.

Under **Alternative 3**, the National Park Service, in conjunction with the US Air Force Museum, would acquire, preserve, and interpret Delta One and Delta Nine as a National Historic Site. The site would commemorate the history and significance of the Minuteman missile system, the Cold War, and the arms race. This alternative received the greatest public support.

VISITOR CENTER ALTERNATIVES

This report also outlines several administrative and interpretive alternatives for a potential Minuteman Missile National Historic Site. If Delta One and Delta Nine become a National Historic Site, the National Park Service could: 1) Construct a "stand-alone" visitor center that focuses on the interpretation of the Minuteman missile and related issues of the Cold War; or 2) Develop a "multi-resource" visitor center that offers information on Minuteman as well as other aspects of Great Plains history and culture, such as Wounded Knee and Chief Big Foot's Trail. These options, as well as possible locations for the visitor center, are discussed at length later in this report.

Department of Defense Legacy Resource Management Program

Funding for the Minuteman Special Resource Study of Delta One and Delta Nine was provided by the Department of Defense Legacy Resource Management Program. The conservation of the Department of Defense's natural and cultural resources has been an important part of the Department's management of its installations throughout its history. This early commitment to resource stewardship has evolved into well-defined, formalized, and integrated natural and cultural resources programs. Today, Department of Defense programs devote more than $30 million to the identification, protection, and enhancement of our Nation's natural and cultural resources.

The Legacy Resource Management Program, which was created by the Department of Defense Appropriation Act of 1991, places special attention on stewardship. The focus is on identifying resources, evaluating their significance within the contexts of natural and cultural resource values such as historic interpretation, and developing preservation techniques that integrate the objectives of the military mission. The Legacy Program is proving that it is possible for the Department of Defense to conduct the national defense mission, reduce costs, improve effectiveness, and enhance public awareness while providing sound stewardship for our Nation's natural and cultural resources.

Criteria for Parklands

Among the alternatives being considered is the possibility of Delta One and Delta Nine becoming a new unit of the National Park Service. The category of designation that would be most appropriate for Delta One and Delta Nine is **National Historic Site**. A National Historic Site preserves a place or commemorates a person, event, or activity important in American history. The management philosophy of the National Park Service is outlined in the Organic Act of 1916, which created the National Park Service. The Organic Act calls for the preservation of America's natural, scenic, and historic resources, and allows for public enjoyment in such a way that will leave those resources unimpaired for future generations.

According to National Park Service policy, any new additions to the park service system must also be evaluated in terms of their **national significance**, **suitability**, and **feasibility**. As such, the Minuteman Special Resource Study Team evaluated Delta One and Delta Nine according to these criteria.

NATIONAL SIGNIFICANCE OF DELTA ONE AND DELTA NINE

A proposed unit to the National Park Service is considered nationally significant if it meets all four of the following standards:

- It is an outstanding example of a particular type of resource.
- It possesses exceptional value or quality in illustrating or interpreting the natural or cultural themes of our Nation's heritage.
- It offers superlative opportunities for recreation, for public use and enjoyment, or for scientific study.
- It retains a high degree of integrity as a true, accurate, and relatively unspoiled example of the resource.

The Minuteman Special Resource Study Team determined that Delta One and Delta Nine meet these standards and are suitable for inclusion in the National Park Service system. The Air Force recently nominated Delta One

---

Left: *The frightening specter of a thermonuclear war prompted thousands of Americans to construct their own bomb shelters during the late 1950s and early 1960s. The Federal Civil Defense Administration provided brochures, containing architectural plans and specifications for bomb shelters, to interested families.* UPI PHOTOGRAPH ENTITLED, "H-BOMB HIDEAWAY" IN GARDEN CITY, NEW YORK, 1955

and Delta Nine as a National Historic Landmark, the nation's highest level of historical designation.

When the Soviet Union began to extend its boundaries and increase its military strength after World War II, many American leaders ascribed these activities to a deep-seated and innately hostile Soviet expansionism. The Soviets would be satisfied, they believed, only when the American way of life had been destroyed and the entire world converted to Communism. In order to halt this process, the United States adopted a policy of "patient but firm . . . containment of Russian expansive tendencies." By the early 1950s, however, the United States also understood that any attempt to confront the ubiquitous Soviet threat by using conventional military forces would be both tremendously expensive and politically unacceptable. Faced with these prospects, American leaders formulated a new strategy. Henceforth, the United States would attempt to deter Communist aggression by threatening immediate and massive retaliation using nuclear weapons.

As the Nation mobilized to implement this strategy during the 1950s, the Air Force developed and deployed a new type of weapon that was capable of delivering a thermonuclear warhead to a target half a world away. This weapon was the intercontinental ballistic missile. General Bernard A. Schriever, who directed the effort, called the ICBM project "the largest military development program ever undertaken by this Nation in peacetime." By the early 1960s, the missile program had helped make the "military-industrial complex" a fact of American economic and social life. Billions of American dollars, hundreds of thousands of American workers, and more than 2,000 American companies were directly involved in the effort to develop and deploy ICBMs.

The Minuteman ICBM system was the culmination of that effort. Powerful, accurate, reliable, and capable of being economically mass produced, the solid-fueled Minuteman missile was the Nation's first truly effective deterrent weapon. Beginning in 1961, the Air Force installed 1,000 Minutemen in under-

Definitions — Is it an LCF, an LCC, or an LF?

As in the case of most specialized fields, Minuteman missileers developed their own "language," filled with code words, acronyms, and abbreviations. For example, the crew referred to missiles as "birds." "Birds in flight" meant launched missiles. Three of the most common abbreviations were LCF, LCC, and LF, which refer to various portions of the missile installation, all of which are represented at Delta One and Delta Nine:

Launch Control Facility (LCF)

An LCF is the entire launch control facility complex. This includes the underground launch control center; a topside support building that has eating and sleeping facilities, a security control center, and various equipment rooms; and a heated garage. Delta One was one of 15 Minuteman LCFs at Ellsworth AFB.

Launch Control Center (LCC)

Located beneath an LCF, the LCC is the underground, pod-like structure that was the operational center of the missile launch system. At Delta One, the LCC is 31 feet below ground and connected to the surface by an elevator. Within the submarine-like atmosphere of the LCC, a two-person crew was on duty 24 hours a day.

Launch Facility (LF)

An LF is the missile silo complex. Delta Nine, which was one of 150 Minuteman LFs at Ellsworth AFB, is comprised of an 80-foot-deep underground missile silo and a separate underground utility support building.

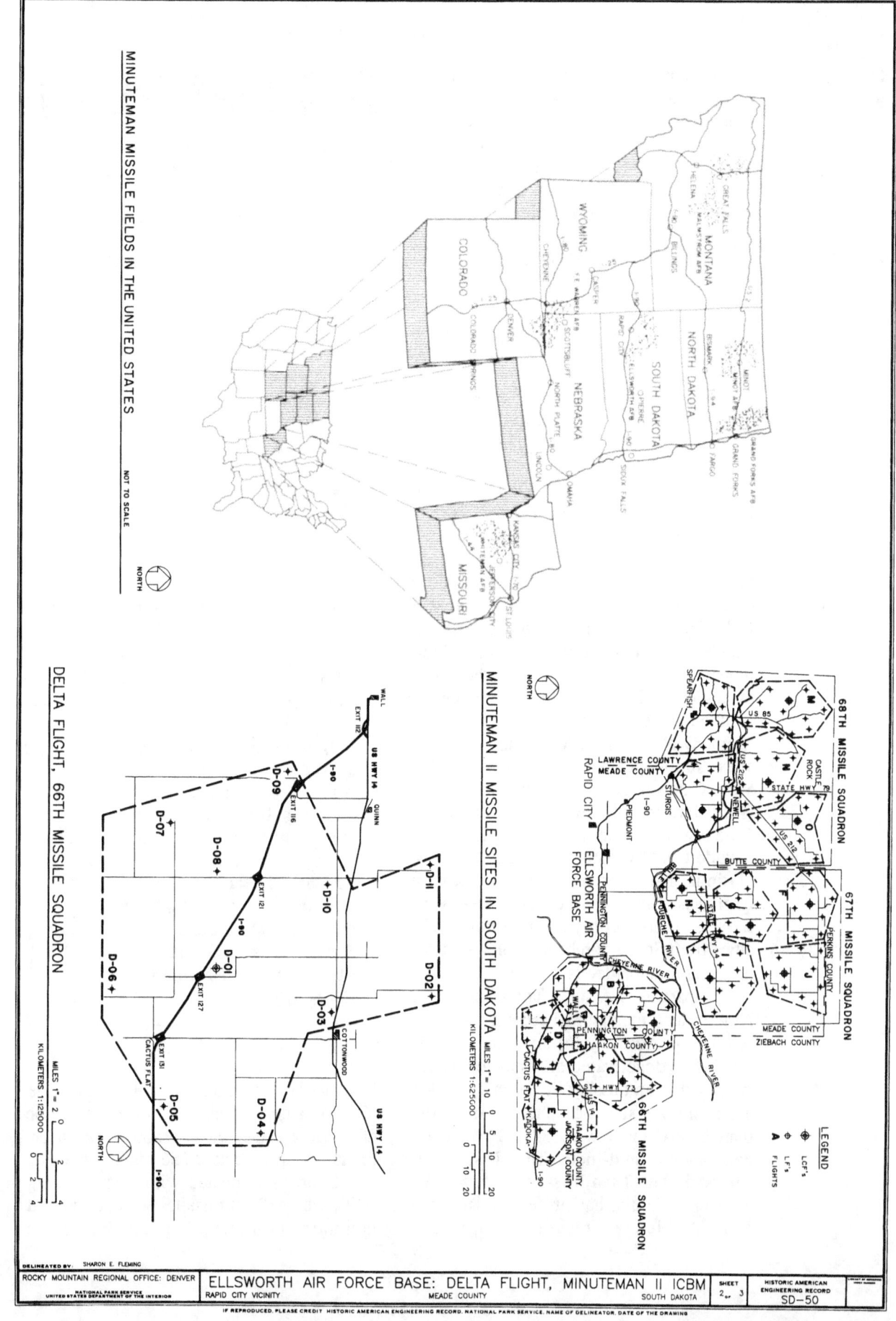

ground launch silos dispersed predominantly throughout the high plains of the central United States. For the next three decades, this force remained on continuous alert — forming the backbone of the American nuclear arsenal, and serving as an important instrument of American diplomacy.

SUITABILITY OF DELTA ONE AND DELTA NINE

To be **suitable**, a site must possess national significance and represent a theme or type of resource that is not already adequately represented in the National Park Service system, or is not comparably represented and protected for public enjoyment by another land-managing entity.

As noted above, Delta One and Delta Nine possess national significance. In addition, the Minuteman Special Resource Study team determined that the National Park Service does not have a unit that specifically commemorates or interprets the Cold War. Delta One and Delta Nine could fill this gap. The National Park Service system includes units associated with presidents who served during the Cold War, including the Harry S Truman, Eisenhower, and John Fitzgerald Kennedy National Historic Sites, but these sites do not specifically interpret the Cold War. Gateway National Recreation Area (New Jersey and New York) and Golden Gate National Recreation Area (California) include Cold War structures. But these two National Park Service units only contain fragments of Nike missile batteries — which the US Army deployed to defend major cities from Soviet bombers — and are interpreted at minimal levels.

Comparative sites to Delta One and Delta Nine include the first and second-generation ICBMs — Atlas, Titan, and Titan II. The Air Force deactivated all first-generation Atlas and Titan missiles by the end of 1965. These missile sites were then partially dismantled and many were sold. Two second-generation, liquid-fueled Titan II sites have survived. The Titan Missile Museum near Tucson, Arizona, has preserved Titan Site 571-7, which was recently designated a National Historic Landmark. But Titan Site 571-7 was compromised by the construction of a visitor center directly above the underground control center. The other Titan site, 395 Charlie, is located within Vandenberg AFB, where Titan missiles were tested and maintained on alert. The Air Force has

Vicinity Map ▶

Delta One and Delta Nine are in southwestern South Dakota, an area already rich with natural and cultural attractions. The sites are in the vicinity of Badlands National Park, which is approximately 70 miles east of Rapid City. Mount Rushmore National Memorial and Black Hills National Forest are to the west. Other regional attractions include Jewel Cave National Monument, Wind Cave National Park, Deadwood National Historic Landmark, and Buffalo Gap National Grassland.

Located between the communities of Wall and Cactus Flat, the Delta One and Delta Nine missile facilities are adjacent to Interstate 90, which is a major east-west tourist route. Delta One is in Jackson County, approximately 1.7 miles north of Interstate 90 on County Road CS 23A at Exit 127. Delta Nine is in Pennington County, one-half mile south of Interstate 90 on Buffalo Gap National Grassland Road 7116 at Exit 116.

Built in accordance with Air Force dispersal strategy, Delta One and Delta Nine are approximately 11 miles apart, and were linked together through a system of blastproof underground cables and a radio communications network. Delta One and Delta Nine were part of a ten-missile operational unit (Delta Flight) assigned to the 66th Strategic Missile Squadron of the 44th Missile Wing, headquartered at Ellsworth AFB.

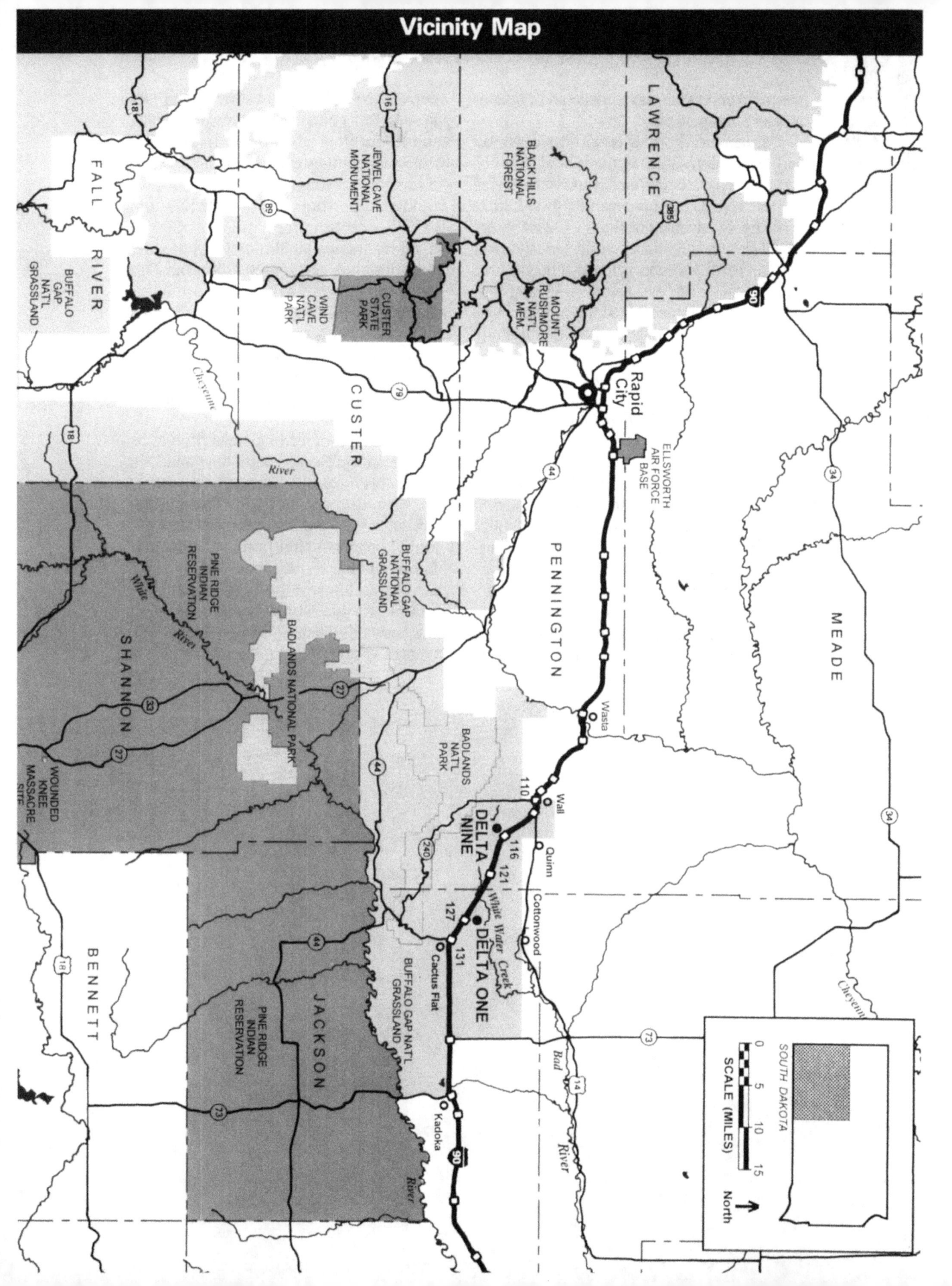

restricted access to this test site and provides limited interpretation.

Whiteman AFB in Missouri has deactivated and preserved a Minuteman II launch control center: Oscar One. But Oscar One is not a "typical" Minuteman facility. Unlike all other Minuteman facilities — which were dispersed in rural areas outside the confines of Air Force bases to increase their chances for surviving a nuclear attack — Oscar One is on a military base. In addition, Oscar One is a more modern version of Minuteman, significantly different from the Cuban Missile Crisis-era configuration of Delta One.

FEASIBILITY OF DELTA ONE AND DELTA NINE

To be **feasible** as a unit of the National Park Service, a site's natural systems and/or historic settings must be of sufficient size and appropriate configuration to ensure long-term protection and accommodate public use. It must also have the potential for efficient administration at a reasonable cost.

The Minuteman Special Resource Study Team determined that the large amount of Federally-owned property surrounding Delta One and Delta Nine would provide sufficient land to develop a National Historic Site, while maintaining existing natural systems and historic settings. Additional property could also be transferred to the National Park Service from the US Forest Service, which has major landholdings in the area. The primary threat to Delta One and Delta Nine is the potential for development of adjacent lands in ways that might intrude on the historic character of either site. However, the National Park Service could alleviate these threats through the use of scenic easements or land trades that would protect the sites' historic character.

The creation of a Minuteman Missile National Historic Site at Delta One and Delta Nine is also feasible because of the missile sites' location near a major thoroughfare (Interstate 90), the potential for employees from the regional labor force, and the availability of utilities in the area within the next few years. These factors would make it possible for the National Park Service to efficiently administer a Minuteman Missile National Historic Site at a reasona-ble cost.

. . . we have been compelled to create a permanent armaments industry of vast proportions. Added to this, three and a half million men and women are directly engaged in the defense establishment. We annually spend on military security more than the net income of all United States corporations. This conjunction of an immense military establishment and a large arms industry is new in the American experience. The total influence — economic, political, even spiritual — is felt in every city, every State house, every office of the Federal Government.

— President Dwight D. Eisenhower

"Farewell Radio and Television Address to the American People"
January 17, 1961

History of the Minuteman ICBM Missile System

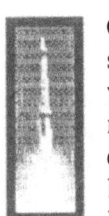 On October 4, 1957, the Soviet Union successfully launched into orbit the world's first artificial satellite, Sputnik. Ham radio operators in the eastern United States turned their dials to lower frequency bands and anxiously listened as the 184-pound Sputnik emitted a mechanical "... beep ... beep ... beep ..." while passing overhead. Other radio operators quickly recorded the broadcast and, within hours, Americans in their living rooms heard Sputnik's transmission via radio and television news flashes. The message seemed to confirm America's worst fears: the Soviets had technologically surpassed the United States and gained supremacy of outer space. The Soviet scientific community wasted little time boasting about their apparent win. Immediately after the launch, one Muscovite scientist commented, "Americans design better automobile tailfins, but we design the best intercontinental ballistic missiles and earth satellites." In the United States, one headline proclaimed: "U.S. Must Catch Up with Reds or We're Dead."

In truth, the significance of the successful launching was not so much Sputnik, but the huge Soviet rocket that hurled the satellite into space. With Sputnik, which is Russian for "fellow traveler," the Soviets demonstrated the ability of their SS-6 launcher to propel a missile toward a target thousands of miles away. Four years earlier, the Soviets exploded the "H-bomb." Now, the frightening prospect of a Soviet missile delivering a nuclear bomb to an American city in less than an hour revived what some called a "Pearl Harbor atmosphere" throughout the United States. At the urging of his military advisors and under tremendous public pressure, President Dwight D. Eisenhower reluctantly accelerated America's ICBM program.

The shock of Sputnik abruptly reversed what

Note: *This history has been adapted from the National Historic Landmark nomination that was prepared for Delta One and Delta Nine in 1994 by John F. Lauber, a historian with Hess, Roise and Company, Minneapolis, Minnesota.*

Left: *Listening to Sputnik I radio signals, ham radio operators Dick Oberholtzer and wife in Elm Grove, Wisconsin, hear beeps every second, October 1957.* LIFE MAGAZINE

Vice President Richard M. Nixon, President Dwight D. Eisenhower, and Secretary of State John Foster Dulles (left to right) at the Brown Palace Hotel, Denver, Colorado, August 1952.

Air Force Secretary Donald Quarles had characterized as America's "poor man's approach" to the ICBM program. Within six months after Sputnik, the Nation's space research and development budget mushroomed from an average half billion dollars a year to more than $10.5 billion. Much of the money went to the development of the Minuteman missile. In 1958, Congress increased the appropriation for Minuteman from $50 to $140 million. The following year, Congress added two billion dollars to the Minuteman budget, to be spread out over the next five years.

Sputnik sparked the development and deployment of the Minuteman missile. But the origins of the Minuteman missile program were deeply rooted in the years immediately following World War II — when the world's two superpowers began to engage in the spiralling arms race of the Cold War.

ORIGINS OF THE ARMS RACE

On January 7, 1954, President Eisenhower delivered his first State of the Union address to the Nation. After declaring that "American freedom is threatened so long as the Communist conspiracy exists in its present scope, power and hostility," the President outlined his plans for defending the Nation against that threat. "We will not be aggressors," he said, "but we . . . have and will maintain a massive capability to strike back." Eisenhower's comments reflected the doctrinal basis behind much of America's strategic planning during the Cold War era.

President Eisenhower's view of the Soviet Union was similar to one that had been articulated nearly eight years earlier by George Kennan, a diplomat at the US embassy in Moscow. Watching the Soviets surround themselves with a "buffer zone" that included much of eastern Europe following World War II, Kennan had argued that these moves resulted from a fanatical Soviet "expansionism" that was ultimately bent on disrupting American society, destroying the American way of life, and breaking the international authority of America. The only way to deal with this threat, Kennan suggested, was for the United States to adopt a policy of "patient but firm and vigilant containment of Russian expansive tendencies."

Although good in theory, containment proved nearly impossible to put into practice. In order to truly contain the pervasive Soviet threat, observed one top US official in 1954, the Nation would need to prepare for combat "in the Arctic and in the tropics; in Asia, in the near East and in Europe; by sea, by land, and by air." But while the Soviet Union had mounted a massive effort to rebuild its army and replenish conventional weapons after World War II, America had demobilized at a dizzying rate. Exploiting its position as the sole possessor of the atomic bomb, the United States pursued what some observers called a "bargain-basement" defense policy, using nuclear weapons as stand-ins for foot soldiers.

Fiscally conservative, President Eisenhower also wanted to keep America's atomic arsenal to the minimum amount necessary to deter Moscow. The President and his chief economic advisor, Arthur H. Burns, believed that the Federal government needed to cut spending, reduce taxes, and balance the budget in order to achieve steady economic growth. Despite protests from the Joint Chiefs of Staff, Eisenhower continually pressed for large cuts in military spending, which consumed almost 70% of the national budget at the time he took office in 1953.

THE AMERICAN ICBM PROGRAM

American military planners began developing ballistic missiles immediately after World War II. But by the late 1940s, America's missile program began to languish, largely because the Nation's nuclear superiority seemed secure. In 1949, when the Soviet Union developed its atomic bomb, America responded with an even more powerful weapon — a thermonuclear device that used a small atomic trigger to initiate a fusion reaction in hydrogen isotopes. Successfully tested in 1952, the H-bomb seemed to guarantee America's nuclear superiority. But in August 1953, the Soviets exploded their own H-bomb, and many US military experts also believed that the Soviets could deliver their new weapon via an ICBM. For the first time, the Soviets seemed poised to take the lead in the arms race.

Following the Soviet's successful H-bomb test, two independent US organizations reevaluated the strategic importance of ICBMs to national security. As Dr. Bruno Augenstein of the RAND Corporation observed, "If the Soviet Union beat the United States in a race for the ICBM, the consequences would be cata-

Air Force Assistant Secretary for Research and Development Trevor Gardner (left) and Maj. General Bernard A. Schriever (right) were key players in the development of intercontinental ballistic missiles, including the Minuteman.

strophic." An Air Force committee headed by Dr. John von Neumann, a Princeton University mathematics professor, also assessed the arms race. Code-named the "Teapot Committee," von Neumann's group investigated "the impact of the thermonuclear [bomb] on the development of strategic missiles and the possibility that the Soviet Union might be somewhat ahead of the United States." In February 1954, RAND and the Teapot Committee released their reports, both of which reached the same conclusion: recent advances in thermonuclear technology made an ICBM practical. Furthermore, an ICBM "could be developed and deployed early enough to counter the pending Soviet threat *if* exceptional talents, adequate funds and new management techniques suited to the urgency of the situation were authorized."

By May 1954, the Air Force had mapped out a development plan for the new weapon. In June, Vice Chief of Staff General Thomas D. White ordered the Air Research and Development Command "to proceed with the devel-

COLD WAR

1945
Bombing of Hiroshima and Nagasaki

1946
Churchill's *iron curtain* speech

1947
Truman Doctrine

1948
Communist coup in Czechoslovakia / Berlin Blockade begins

1949
NATO established / USSR explodes atomic bomb / Communist takeover in China

1950
Sino-Soviet Pact / Korean War begins

1952
US explodes H-bomb

1953
USSR explodes H-bomb

1954
Communist Party outlawed in US

1955
Warsaw Pact / First US civil defense exercise

1956
Hungarian uprising / Krushchev tells the US: *We will bury you*

1957
Sputnik

1958
Eisenhower authorizes Minuteman Missile Program

1959
Cuban Revolution

1960
U-2 spy plane shot down by USSR

1961
Bay of Pigs / Berlin Wall built / Eisenhower warns of *military-industrial complex* / **First successful Minuteman test flight**

Above graphics courtesy of: Smithsonian Institution (explosion); *Detroit Free Press* (cartoon); Western History Dept., Denver Public Library, (Eisenhower); and US Air Force (Minuteman flight).

TIME LINE

1962
Cuban Missile Crisis /
Minuteman I goes on alert

1963
Hot line links US and USSR /
Limited Test Ban Treaty

1964
China detonates atomic bomb

1966
Minuteman II goes on alert

1968
Soviet invasion of Czechoslovakia

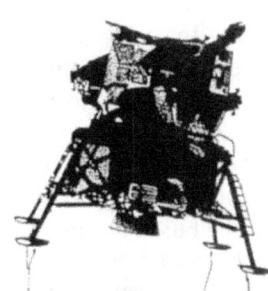

1969
US landing on moon

1970
Minuteman III goes on alert

1972
SALT I agreement

1973
Yom Kippur War: US goes on worldwide alert

1979
SALT II agreement

1983
Reagan proposes *Star Wars* Strategic Defense Initiative (SDI)

1989
Eastern European nations break with Moscow / Berlin Wall comes down

1991
Bush and Gorbachev sign START treaty / **Minuteman II system begins deactivating**

1993
66th Missile Squadron, including Delta Flight, inactivated

In accordance with the START treaty, an Ellsworth AFB transporter-erector vehicle and crew prepare to remove the Minuteman missile from the Delta Nine Launch Facility.

Above graphics courtesy of: Western History Dept., Denver Public Library, (Kennedy); AP/Wide World Photos (protesters, Bush & Gorbachev); Sayre Hutchison (transporter-erector vehicle).

opment of an ICBM at the highest speed possible, limited only by the advancement of technology in the various fields concerned." In July, the Air Force established a special project office to administer the program. Based on the West Coast, the new agency was consequently called the Western Development Division. Bernard A. Schriever, a 43-year-old brigadier general, headed Western Development Division. The Air Force expected the newly-promoted young general to place a fully operational ICBM weapon system into the hands of the Strategic Air Command within six years. The Air Force considered Western Development Division's mission so important to national security that even its initials, WDD, were classified beyond top secret.

On August 5, 1954, General Schriever and a small group of military officers converged on an abandoned parochial school in the Los Angeles suburb of Inglewood to begin their work. To avoid arousing the curiosity of nearby residents, the officers wore civilian clothes. Journalist Roy Neal, who chronicled the development of the Minuteman missile system, described what they found:

> *No sign identified the white schoolhouse as the Western Development Division.
> . . . The windows were frosted and heavily barred. All outside doors, except one, were locked. The only entrance was across a chain-link fenced parking lot. A security guard manned the door. . . . Some of the old-timers recall . . . the comment of the school boy who was sauntering by the school building. Eying the frosted glass and steel-barred windows, he said to a chum, "Boy am I glad I don't go to school here."*

In this inconspicuous but carefully secured setting, the hand-picked staff of the Western Development Division began the effort to build an intercontinental ballistic missile.

FIRST GENERATION ICBMs: ATLAS and TITAN

The Western Development Division staff began its work by reviving a missile project

German V-2 missiles, which Adolph Hitler hailed as Vergeltungswaffe (vengeance weapons), were used against the Allies during the closing years of World War II.

that had originated shortly after World War II. In 1946, the Air Force had contracted with the Convair Corporation to design a long-range ballistic missile called the MX-774. Like many post-war missile projects, the MX-774 lost most of its government funding after only one year. But, instead of dropping the project, Convair Corporation continued working on its own, steadily advancing the state of missile technology. In 1951, the Air Force acknowledged these efforts by hiring the company to develop plans for a more advanced missile, called the Atlas.

The Atlas was essentially a highly evolved version of the German V-2 missile, which Germany had used against the Allies during the waning years of World War II. Like the V-2, the Atlas was powered by rocket engines that burned a mixture of liquid fuel and oxidizer. But while the V-2 had an effective range of only a few hundred miles, the Atlas had to deliver its payload to a target more than 5,000 miles away. Convair Corporation could have met this requirement by designing the Atlas as an enormous version of the V-2. Instead, Convair's engineers sought a more sophisticated solution. Realizing that a missile's range could be increased by reducing its weight, Convair equipped the Atlas with an innovative, ultra-light airframe. Convair assembled the missile from rings of paper-thin stainless steel, stacked together like stovepipes and welded at the seams to form cylinders. The cylinders were then inflated with nitrogen gas to give the missile its structural integrity.

By 1954, the Atlas was the Nation's most advanced ballistic missile. Nonetheless, the

Atlas missile awaiting test launch from Cape Canaveral on Christmas Eve, 1958. **Inset:** *Test launch of the Atlas D missile. The development of the solid-fueled Minuteman missile accelerated the early retirement of the first generation of liquid-fueled ICBMs, such as the Atlas D and Atlas E, which the Air Force deactivated by 1965.*

missile was years away from production. No prototype had been flight tested, and some skeptics feared that when Atlas's powerful engines were fired for the first time, the missile's thin-skinned airframe would buckle in on itself, leaving America's hopes for an ICBM lying on the launch pad like a gigantic ball of tin foil.

General Schriever and his staff were aware of these concerns. So while they proceeded with the Atlas program, they also looked for a backup. In October 1955, the Air Force contracted with the Glenn L. Martin Company to produce a new ICBM called the Titan. Like the Atlas, the Titan used liquid propellants, but its advanced two-stage design allowed for a conventional, and more reliable, airframe.

Still, America's missile program was hampered by funding problems. In 1956, Air Force Secretary Donald Quarles rejected the operational budget for the ICBM program, and proposed the elimination of either Atlas or Titan, which he considered redundant. That same year, the Air Force lost its most effective missile proponent when Assistant Secretary Trevor Gardner, the "Missile Czar," announced his retirement, citing continued cuts to his missile research and development budgets. Undeterred by Gardner's retirement, Quarles's austerity campaign continued into 1957 when the ballistic missile program was slashed by $200 million. In July, the Eisenhower administration initiated even more cost-saving measures, including cutting missile deliveries, lowering overtime rates, and delaying payments to contractors.

STRENGTH IN NUMBERS: THE MISSILE GAP

This frugal economic climate changed dramatically after Sputnik. In October 1957, when the Soviet Union announced it had used a liquid-fueled ICBM to launch Sputnik into orbit, American scientists and politicians feared a significant "missile gap." Within months, journalists and intelligence analysts began asserting that the Soviet missile force could outnumber the American arsenal by as much as 16 to one by 1960. America's growing sense of insecurity was not lost on Soviet officials, who

Titan I test launch, Vandenberg Air Force Base, May 4, 1962. The Titan missile possessed a greater range and bigger payload than Atlas. Still, the Titan was equally short lived. All Titan missiles were deactivated by June 1965.

gleefully announced that their factories were turning out missiles "like sausages." Facing severe criticism for allowing the United States to fall behind in the arms race, the Eisenhower administration poured more money into its missile programs — increasing the Nation's annual space research and development budget by more than twenty-fold within six months after Sputnik. The administration also highlighted the development of the Atlas and Titan missiles. One government spokesperson noted that America's missile program was being carefully designed, first to "attain perfection," and then to "develop the ability to produce in volume once that perfection is achieved."

But America's first-generation ICBMs were neither perfect nor mass-producible. A few weeks after Sputnik, the *Wall Street Journal* observed that the weaknesses of America's ICBMs "are so profound that . . . generals are sure [the missiles] will be discarded altogether

Colonel Edward Hall spearheaded the US Air Force effort to develop a solid-fueled ICBM.

after the first half-dozen years." Atlas and Titan were extraordinarily complex, hand-crafted machines, containing as many as 300,000 parts, each of which had to be maintained in perfect operating condition. The liquid propellants that powered the missiles' engines were volatile and corrosive, and could not be placed in the fuel tanks until immediately before launch. In addition, the missile crews needed as much as two hours to fuel the missiles. Consequently, instead of being "stable weapons in a state of permanent readiness," these ICBMs required "the desperate and constant attention accorded a man receiving artificial respiration." The missiles were not a "push button affair but will require a highly-trained crew . . . several times as large as the largest bombing crew." Many of these problems could be solved, the *Wall Street Journal* suggested, by developing a simplified "second generation" of missiles powered by solid-fuel rocket engines.

"A lot of work had been done on solids prior to the initiation of the ICBM program in 1954," recalled General Schriever in a 1973 interview, "but there were a number of things that ruled against using solids at that time."

Solid propellants in the mid-1950s could not provide enough power to hurl a thermonuclear warhead across an ocean. Also, solids were difficult to manufacture. They were hard to ignite, and there was no way to control their combustion or direct their thrust after ignition. Given these constraints, the Air Force believed that liquid-fueled missiles were "the only immediate way to go ahead." But the Air Force did not entirely abandon the concept of a solid-fuel missile. In 1956, Schriever reluctantly approved a low-level research program "aimed toward the evolution of a high-thrust . . . solid-fuel rocket." Schriever selected Colonel Edward Hall, Chief of Propulsion Development for the Western Development Division, to head the program. According to historian Robert Perry, Hall was a "near-fanatic" about the potential of solid-fuel missiles.

WEAPON SYSTEM "Q"

Colonel Edward Hall and his staff of engineers diligently researched their solid-fuel missile program. Within two years, Hall's group had solved most of the problems associated with solid-fuel rocket engines. In August 1957, the Air Force asked Hall to develop a medium-range, solid-fuel missile to be the land-based counterpart to the Navy's submarine-launched, solid-fuel Polaris. Within two weeks, Hall drew up specifications for a remarkable new missile whose range could be varied by simply assembling its three interchangeable propulsion stages in different combinations.

The new missile, dubbed "Weapon System Q," was "the first strategic weapon capable of true mass production," wrote Duke University historian George Reed. "To Hall, the new missile was the perfect weapon for a defense policy characterized by minimum expenditure and massive retaliation; and he urged that this be its chief selling point." Sputnik made it easy for Colonel Hall to make the sale. A few days after the Sputnik launch, Hall went to the Pentagon with General Schriever to build support for the new missile. As they ascended the ranks of the military hierarchy, Hall refined his plans. By the end of 1957, he determined that "the ICBM version of Weapon System Q

would be a three-stage, solid-fuel missile approximately 65 feet long, weighing approximately 65,000 pounds, and developing approximately 100,000-120,000 pounds of thrust at launch." The missile would be stored vertically in underground silos and "would accelerate so quickly that it could fly through its exhaust flames and not be significantly damaged."

In February 1958, Hall and Schriever presented Weapon System Q to the Secretaries of the Air Force and Defense. "We got approval . . . within 48 hours," Schriever recalled. The officers immediately renamed the project. On February 28, 1958, the *New York Times* reported that the Air Force had been authorized "to produce an advanced type of ballistic missile . . . called Minute Man."

MINUTEMAN I

By the end of March 1958, at least seven of the Nation's foremost aircraft manufacturers, including the Boeing Airplane Company, were competing to build the new missile. Although Seattle-based Boeing had built many of the Nation's largest strategic bombers, the company had virtually no experience with missiles. Still, Boeing mounted an all-out effort to win the Minuteman contract, assigning more than 100 employees to work on the project. When the Air Force selection board met to examine the proposals, one top official recalled that "there was no question . . . that Boeing was the right company for the job." In October 1958, the US government contracted with Boeing to assemble and test the new missile.

During the next few months, the rest of the Minuteman missile team came into place. The Thiokol Chemical Company of Brigham City, Utah, the Aerojet General Corporation of Sacramento, California, and the Hercules Powder Company of Magna, Utah, all won contracts to work on the missile's propulsion stages. Minuteman's guidance and control systems went to the Autonetics Division of North American Aviation in Downey, California. The AVCO Corporation of Boston contracted to build the missile's thermonuclear warhead.

Much of the development work for Minuteman took place in northern Utah. Thiokol and Hercules already operated plants in the area and, within a few months, Boeing moved into a new assembly plant that occupied 790 acres at Hill Air Force Base near Ogden. By the beginning of 1960, Boeing's Minuteman work force had grown to nearly 12,000, as the company started to assemble the missiles. *Time* magazine reported that the desert north of Salt Lake was "boiling" with activity:

Strange lights glare in the night, making the mountains shine, and a grumbling roar rolls across the desert. By day enormous clouds of steam-white smoke billow up . . . and drift over hills and valleys. Monstrous vehicles with curious burdens lumber along the roads. All these strange goings-on mark the development of the Minuteman, the solid-fuel missile that its proponents confidently expect will ultimately replace the liquid-fuel Atlas as the U.S.'s standard ICBM.

Above: *Minuteman I test launch.* **Inset:** *A Minuteman ICBM, ready for testing at the Air Force Missile Test Center, Cape Canaveral, Florida.*

According to journalist Roy Neal, the ICBM program created a new national industry: "Tens of thousands of industrial and Air Force managers, engineers, and workers [had] to be trained. New machine tools and test facilities [had to] come into being. . . ." These efforts changed "the face of America, the make-up of the Armed Forces and the industries that support them."

At the end of 1960, the Air Force took the first Minuteman missile to Cape Canaveral, Florida, for flight testing. The compact new missile was only six feet in diameter and 53 feet high — about half the size of a Titan. Minuteman's three cylindrical, steel-cased propulsion stages were stacked one atop the other, with each stage slightly smaller in diameter than the one beneath it. Each stage was filled with a rubbery mixture of fuel and oxidizer, molded around a hollow, star-shaped core. The Minuteman's guidance system occupied a small compartment above the third stage. The "reentry vehicle" at the tip was identical to the nosecone that would eventually contain a thermonuclear warhead.

Following two aborted launch attempts, the Air Force successfully fired the first Minuteman missile at 11:00 a.m. on February 1, 1961. Even the most experienced missile watchers found it to be "a dazzling spectacle." When the missile's first-stage engine ignited, there was a loud bang. Then the missile began to rise on a column of flame and smoke. Unlike the Atlas or Titan missile, which one observer said left the ground "like a fat man getting out of an easy chair," the Minuteman

missile "shot up like a skyrocket." The missile performed flawlessly. The three propulsion stages completed their burns on schedule, then detached themselves and plummeted back to earth, while the unarmed warhead hurled on toward its assigned destination. Twenty-five minutes after liftoff, the reentry vehicle splashed down in the Atlantic Ocean squarely on target — 4,600 miles away.

From his office in Washington D.C., Air Force Chief of Staff General Thomas D. White described the launch as "one of the most significant steps this Nation has ever taken toward gaining intercontinental missile supremacy." An engineer who witnessed the event put it another way: "Brother," he said, "there goes the missile gap."

THE "UNDERGROUND" AIR FORCE

By the time the flight test took place, the Air Force was already planning for Minuteman missile deployment. According to historian Jacob Neufeld, the Air Force conceptually developed its "ideal" ICBM base in 1955, during the early days of the Atlas program:

The missile would be sited inside fixed, underground facilities; it was to have a quick launch reaction; it was to be stored in a launching position; the launch site would require minimal support; and the launch units were to be self-supporting for two weeks.

Turning these ideas into reality, however, proved difficult. During the height of the "missile gap" hysteria, the Air Force hastily activated the Nation's first Atlas missiles at Vandenberg Air Force Base in California. Here, the Air Force stored the missiles horizontally in "coffins" — concrete-walled, above-ground enclosures. Before the missiles could be fired, servicemen had to raise each missile vertically on a launch pad and add fuel. The later Titan and Atlas F series missiles were stored upright in underground silos capped with massive "clamshell" doors. But Air Force engineers were worried that vibrations from the rocket engines might shake the missiles apart before launch. As a result, the Air Force equipped each silo with an elevator that raised the missile to the surface for firing. Although the missiles were stored with their tanks full of fuel, workers still needed to add volatile liquid oxygen right before launch.

The Air Force took a major step toward achieving its ideal basing system in 1960 with the development of Titan II, which used storable liquid propellants. The Air Force could store Titan II missiles with fully-loaded propellant tanks, and fire them directly from underground silos. Nonetheless, Titan II missiles still needed constant attention from an on-site crew.

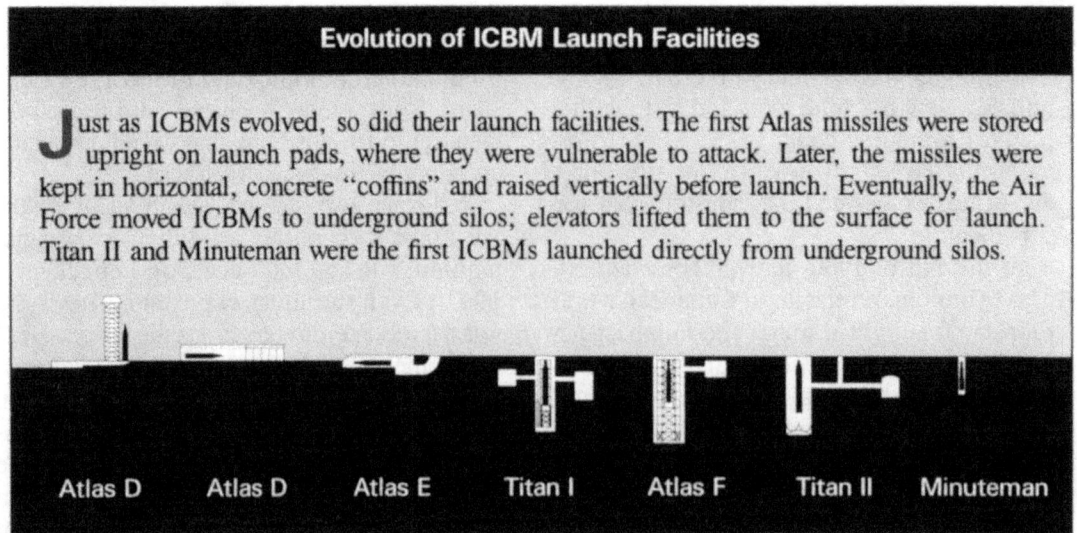

Evolution of ICBM Launch Facilities

Just as ICBMs evolved, so did their launch facilities. The first Atlas missiles were stored upright on launch pads, where they were vulnerable to attack. Later, the missiles were kept in horizontal, concrete "coffins" and raised vertically before launch. Eventually, the Air Force moved ICBMs to underground silos; elevators lifted them to the surface for launch. Titan II and Minuteman were the first ICBMs launched directly from underground silos.

Atlas D   Atlas D   Atlas E   Titan I   Atlas F   Titan II   Minuteman

When Minuteman was added to the Nation's arsenal, America acquired its first truly push-button — literally *turn-key* — missile system. Historian Ernest Schwiebert noted:

With the successful utilization of solid propellants, the Minuteman could hide in its lethal lair like a shotgun shell, ready for instant firing. The operational launcher could be unmanned, underground, and hardened to withstand the surface burst of a nuclear weapon. Each launcher housed a single weapon and the equipment necessary to support and fire it, and required only periodic maintenance. The missiles could be fired . . . at a moment's notice.

MINUTEMAN DEPLOYMENT AND SITE SELECTION

The Air Force wanted to deploy Minuteman as a single, immense, "missile farm," equipped with as many as 1,500 missiles. However, the Air Force soon determined that "for reasons of economy 150 launchers should be concentrated in a single area, whenever possible, and that no area should contain fewer than 50 missiles." Consequently, the Air Force organized the Minuteman force into a series of administrative units called "wings," each comprised of three or four 50-missile squadrons. Each squadron was further subdivided into five smaller units, called "flights." A flight consisted of a single, manned, launch control facility, linked to ten, unmanned, underground, missile silos. The silos were separated from the launch control facility and from each other by a distance of several miles.

The Air Force initially considered putting Minuteman missiles as far south as Georgia, Texas, and Oklahoma. But when early models of Minuteman missiles fell short of their intended 5,500-mile range, the Air Force selected sites in the northern part of the United States, which was closer to the Soviet Union. In 1960, the Air Force decided to locate the first Minuteman installation on the high plains around Great Falls, Montana, at Malmstrom AFB. In the event of a nuclear accident or attack, the low population density near Malmstrom AFB

President John F. Kennedy (center), accompanied by Secretary of Defense Robert McNamara (far left), SAC Commander General Thomas S. Power (right), and Lt. General Howell M. Estes, Jr. (right background) at Vandenberg Air Force Base, March 1962.

would minimize civilian casualties. In addition, the region offered an established network of roads and, like much of the West, a large amount of easy-to-acquire public land.

The Air Force began constructing the Nation's first Minuteman missile field on March 16, 1961. In the spring of 1962, the *Associated Press* reported that the Montana silos were being "rushed to completion," and that the first missiles, each loaded with "one megaton of death and destruction," would be ready by late summer. Air Force crews began lowering the weapons into the silos at the end of July, and Malmstrom AFB's first ten-missile flight was hurriedly activated on October 27, 1962, at the height of the Cuban Missile Crisis.

MINUTEMAN COMES TO ELLSWORTH AIR FORCE BASE

Military strategists began planning for a second Minuteman installation shortly after work got underway at Malmstrom AFB. In

June 1960, the Air Force was authorized to add another 150 missiles to the Minuteman force. By early October, military strategists had narrowed their search for a new site to three locations in North and South Dakota. On January 5, 1961, US Senator Francis Case of South Dakota announced that Ellsworth AFB would be the headquarters for the Nation's second Minuteman deployment. Located about 12 miles east of Rapid City, Ellsworth AFB was founded in 1941 as the Rapid City Army Air Base. The Air Corps used the airfield to train B-17 bomber crews, and Ellsworth eventually served as home base for many of America's largest strategic bombers. The base was also headquarters for a Titan I missile squadron.

Although the Defense Department had not yet officially authorized the South Dakota Minuteman installation, Senator Case wanted the land acquired immediately so there would be "no loss of valuable time" once the project was approved. Local ranchers did not share Case's sense of urgency. Fearing that the government might offer below-market prices for their land, the ranchers established the Missile Area Landowners' Association to negotiate fair prices. The association assured fellow citizens that its actions would "not necessarily slow the national defense effort."

While real estate negotiations were underway, the South Dakota State Highway Department spent $650,000 from the Federal Bureau of Public Roads to improve 327 miles of roads leading to the proposed missile sites. By June 1961, Boeing was busy improving the infrastructure. Anticipating that the project would bring in more than 3,000 workers, the company raced to build mobile home camps and cafeterias near Wall, Sturgis, Belle Fourche, and Union Center, as well as in Rapid City.

By early summer, more than three-quarters of the local landowners agreed to give the government access to their land. Once the sites were finalized, the Ralph M. Parsons Company, an architectural and engineering firm from Los Angeles, prepared plans for the Minuteman installation. The Air Force assigned responsibility for construction to the US Army Corps of Engineers Ballistic Missile Construction Office. In July 1961, four of the nation's largest construction firms submitted bids for the project. The low bid came from Peter Kiewit Sons Company of Omaha, whose estimate of $56,220,274 was nearly $10 million below government projections.

> ### The 44th Strategic Missile Wing ▶
>
> Typical of all Minuteman installations, the forces at Ellsworth AFB were organized into a *missile wing*. The 44th Strategic Missile Wing at Ellsworth AFB was activated in 1963, and was comprised of three 50-missile *squadrons*: the 66th, 67th, and 68th Strategic Missile Squadrons.
>
> Each squadron was further subdivided into five smaller units, called *flights*. A flight consisted of a single, manned, underground launch control center (LCC), which was linked through a system of underground cables to ten, unmanned, launch facilities (LF). Each LF held one Minuteman missile stored in an underground silo. The silos were separated from the LCC and each other by a distance of several miles.

A SILO A DAY

On September 10, 1961, the groundbreaking ceremony for Ellsworth AFB's Minuteman installations took place at Site L-6 near Bear Butte. The festivities started with a bang. While the Sturgis High School band played, representatives from Boeing, Kiewit, the Corps of Engineers, and Ellsworth AFB set off an explosive charge to begin the excavation.

Despite extreme cold, high winds, and heavy snowfall, construction proceeded at a furious pace through the winter of 1961-62. In mid-December, the Corps of Engineers told reporters that "men are working seven days a week, three shifts a day on Minuteman construction." A Corps spokesman said that crews were "able to dig five silo emplacements simultaneously. Each takes from four to ten days . . ." The first squadron, near Wall, was well underway,

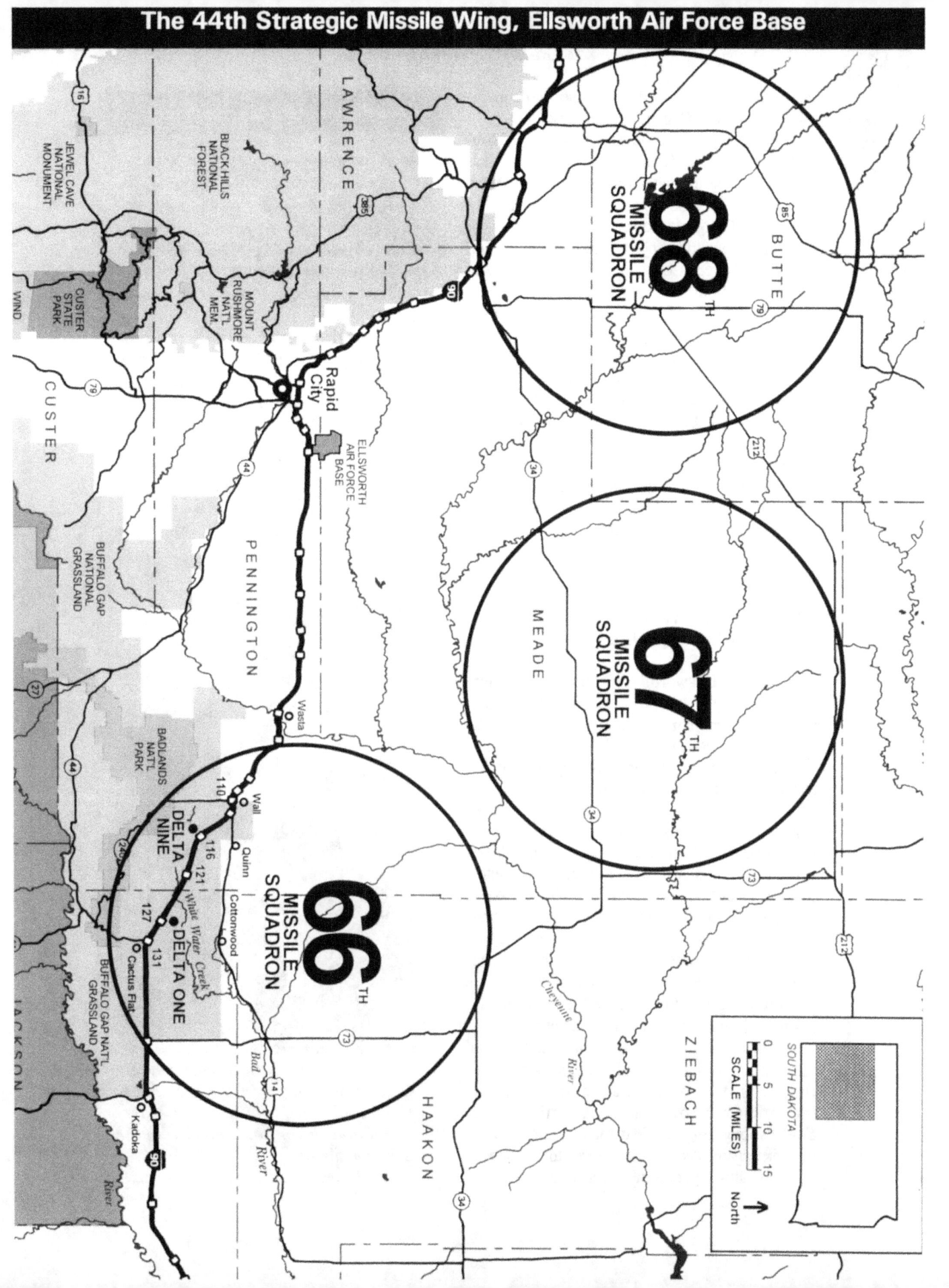

said the Corps, and work on the second squadron, near Union Center, had already started.

In February 1962, General Delmar Wilson told the Rapid City Chamber of Commerce that despite an ongoing labor dispute between Peter Kiewit Sons and the Ironworkers Union, South Dakota's ICBM deployment suffered fewer work stoppages than any missile program in the Nation. "We're all out . . . to assure that our way of life is maintained," stated Wilson. "This missile project . . . is the number one project in the country today. If this guy in Russia wants to start a show, we'll be there to put a hole in him to the best of our ability."

By early summer of 1963, the steel fabrication was finished at all 165 South Dakota sites, and crews were completing the silos at the rate of one per day. On the last day of June, the first 20 silos were turned over to the Strategic Air Command. On October 23, the Nation's second wing of Minuteman ICBMs was fully operational. The work was completed nearly three weeks ahead of schedule.

BACKBONE OF THE US NUCLEAR ARSENAL

While the Ellsworth AFB sites were under construction, the Air Force was building several other Minuteman installations. By the end of 1967, the Nation had 1,000 Minuteman missiles on alert in six separate deployment areas located throughout the north-central United States. In addition to the original installations at Malmstrom AFB and Ellsworth AFB, Minuteman complexes were deployed at Minot AFB and Grand Forks AFB in North Dakota, Whiteman AFB in Missouri, and F.E. Warren AFB in Wyoming. In addition, another squadron was established at Malmstrom AFB. At each installation the Air Force continued to improve and refine the Minuteman operational system.

Newly-elected President John F. Kennedy instigated one of the first significant improvements to the Minuteman weapon system. Soon after taking office in 1961, Kennedy learned that even if he ordered a massive nuclear retaliation to a Soviet attack, a portion of the Soviet's long-range nuclear force would survive to strike again. As a consequence, the Kennedy administration quickly abandoned the strategic

Construction of a Minuteman LF ▶

Peter Kiewit Sons of Omaha, Nebraska, received $56 million from the US Air Force to construct the 150 missile silos and 15 control centers in South Dakota. The *Rapid City Journal* described how a Minuteman silo was built: "Conventional earthmoving equipment scoops an open cut 12 feet deep. A backhoe perches on the edge of a large hole in this cut and digs a hole 20 feet deeper. The remaining 52 feet of depth is 'mined' by a clamshell . . . When each hole is at the full depth of 84 feet, a steel 'can' 12 feet in diameter is carefully positioned in it. Reinforced concrete is poured between the can and earth." Work began on South Dakota's first Minuteman silo on September 10, 1961. By 1963, all 150 launchers were declared fully operational.

"The Spokes of the Wheel"

The Air Force excavated lengthy trenches several miles long to install the underground cables that connected the underground launch control centers with the distant missile silos.

Construction of a Minuteman Launch Facility

1

2

3

4

5

6

> **◄ Construction of a Minuteman LCF**
>
> Delta One's underground launch control center (LCC) was constructed as two separate structural elements. The outside protective shell is 29 feet in diameter and 54 feet in length, and is made of reinforced concrete with four-foot-thick walls. The shell's interior is lined with 1/4-inch-thick steel plate. Suspended inside the shell is the second element: a box-like acoustical enclosure that contains the launch control consoles, communications and monitoring equipment, and crew accommodations. Delta One's "topside" structures include sleeping and eating facilities.

policy of releasing America's entire nuclear arsenal in "one horrific spasm." Instead of massive retaliation, Secretary of Defense Robert McNamara recommended a "flexible response." Should deterrence fail, McNamara proposed that America's nuclear weapons be deployed selectively. The first ICBMs would target enemy bombers and missile sites. The remaining ICBMs would be held in reserve, for potential use against Soviet cities. McNamara hoped that the threat to the civilian population would persuade the Soviet Union to end the conflict. McNamara began retooling America's nuclear forces, including Minuteman, to reflect the new military strategy.

However, Colonel Edward Hall and his engineers designed Minuteman to be a fast-reacting, mass-attack weapon. Upon receiving the launch command, the officers at each Minuteman facility had to fire all ten missiles under their control. A selective launch of fewer than ten missiles was impossible. In order to conform with the new defense strategy, Air Force engineers had to redesign Minuteman's launch control complex. Historian Clyde Littlefield described the changes:

> *In order to conform to the new concept, engineering changes had to be made to allow a combat crew in a control center to switch targets and to fire one or more missiles selectively, conserving the remainder for later use. . . . Greater flexibility in targeting and firing required a significant extension to the limited survival time [of each operational site]. The [original] Minuteman facility design did not provide for the protection of the power supply. . . . At a control center, power generators were above the ground. . . . When and if these generators stopped functioning, the operational potential of the system would be reduced to only six hours. Revised strategic concepts required that the weapon survive at least nine weeks after an initial enemy attack.*

To meet this requirement, the Air Force put the generators in underground capsules next to each launch control center. Although the Air Force considered incorporating these generators into the Minuteman facilities at Ellsworth AFB, construction was already underway there, making the changes impractical. Consequently, the generator capsules began with the third Minuteman deployment area at Minot AFB in North Dakota.

THE NEXT GENERATIONS: MINUTEMAN II AND III

By the time planning began for the final Minuteman deployment area, the Air Force had developed a vastly improved version of the missile. Called Minuteman II, the new missile offered improved range, greater payload, more flexible targeting, and greater accuracy, leading one Air Force spokesperson to estimate that its "kill capacity" was eight times that of Minuteman I. Minuteman II was deployed first at Grand Forks AFB, North Dakota. In September 1965, South Dakota Congressman E.Y. Berry announced that the Ellsworth AFB facilities would also receive the new missile system. According to Berry, Minuteman II would help Ellsworth AFB remain "one of the nation's most important military installations." In October 1971, Boeing began refitting the Ellsworth silos to accommodate Minuteman II, and completed the project in March 1973.

In May 1964, the Soviet Union displayed a

battery of anti-ballistic missiles in Moscow's Red Square, prompting concern about the vulnerability of Minuteman I and II missiles. The following year, the Air Force began to develop an even more advanced version of the missile. By late summer of 1968, Minuteman III was ready for testing. Longer and more powerful than its predecessors, Minuteman III offered an improved guidance system that could be retargeted in minutes. But, according to the *New York Times*, the missile's "most telling advantage" lay in its "revolutionary new warhead: the MIRV, or multiple independently targeted reentry vehicle." The MIRV could deliver three hydrogen bombs to widely scattered targets, a capability that would "render current and contemplated antimissile defense systems largely inadequate," and "thrust the world into a new era of weapons for mass destruction."

The Air Force deployed Minuteman III at Warren, Minot, Grand Forks, and Malmstrom Air Force Bases, and extensively modified the Minuteman launchers at these locations to accommodate the new missiles. Each launch tube was equipped with a new suspension system that could hold the missile absolutely motionless during the aftershocks of a nuclear attack. The Air Force also installed a system of seals, filters, and surge arrestors designed to prevent electronic equipment from being damaged by the powerful electromagnetic waves generated during nuclear explosions.

In July 1975, when the last of the Nation's 550 Minuteman III missiles was lowered into its silo at Malmstrom AFB, Montana, only 450 Minutemen II remained in the American arsenal — at Malmstrom, Ellsworth, and Whiteman Air Force Bases. This force structure remained intact for nearly two more decades.

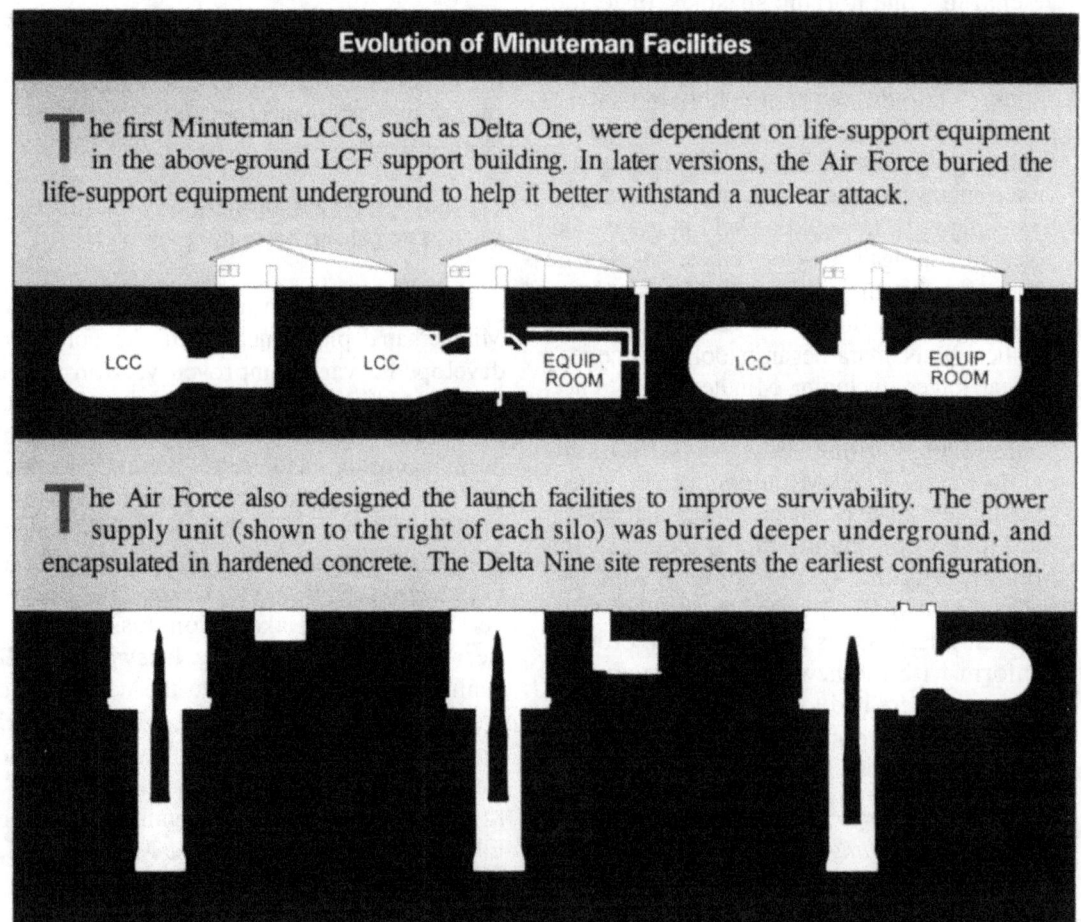

Evolution of Minuteman Facilities

The first Minuteman LCCs, such as Delta One, were dependent on life-support equipment in the above-ground LCF support building. In later versions, the Air Force buried the life-support equipment underground to help it better withstand a nuclear attack.

The Air Force also redesigned the launch facilities to improve survivability. The power supply unit (shown to the right of each silo) was buried deeper underground, and encapsulated in hardened concrete. The Delta Nine site represents the earliest configuration.

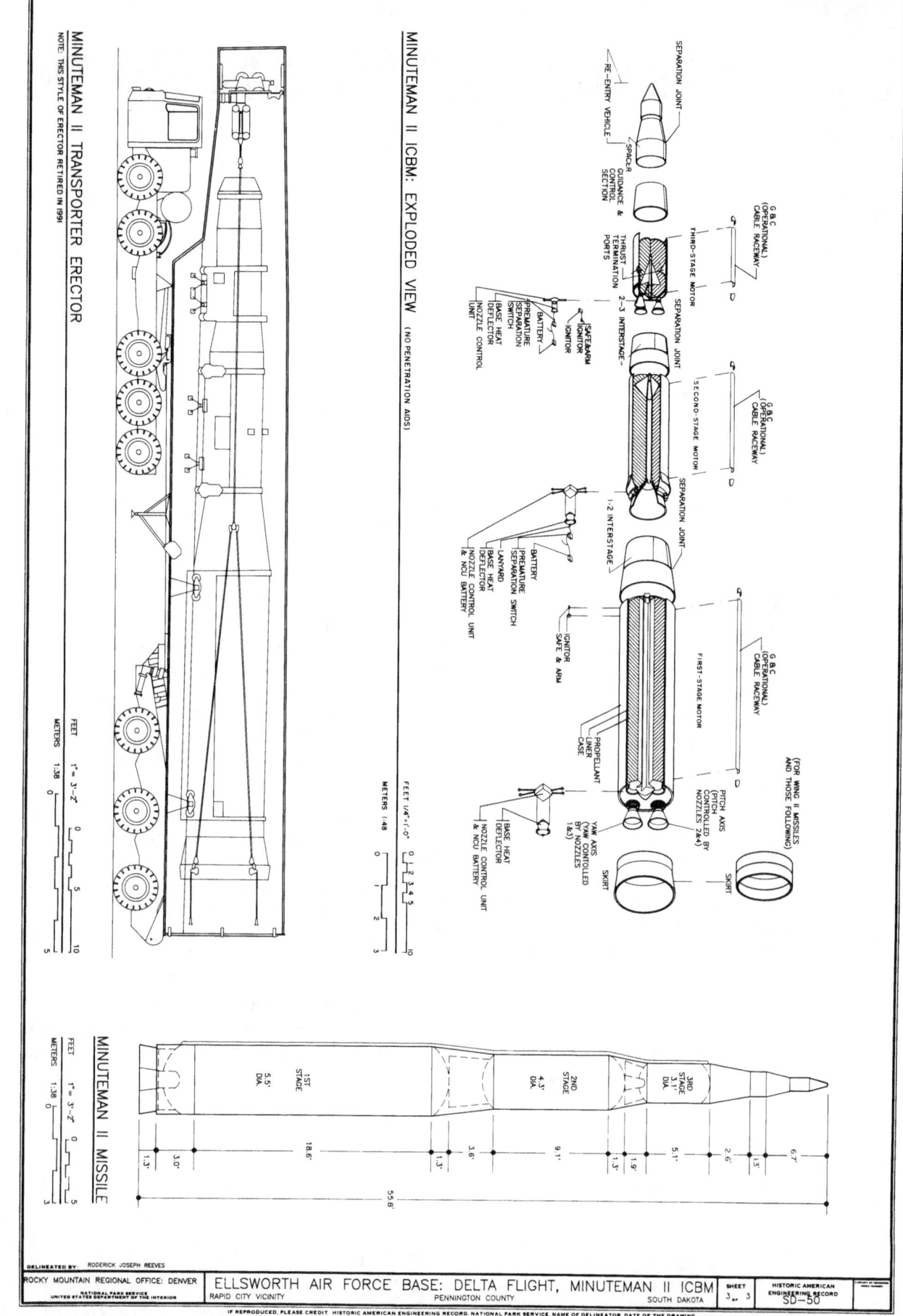

> ### Delta Nine Missile Pull, 1993 ▶
>
> On September 27, 1991, President George Bush announced his "plan for peace," which included the "withdrawal from alert, within 72 hours, of all 450 Minuteman II intercontinental ballistic missiles." The actual physical removal of the missiles began in December 1991, when Air Force crews began pulling the unarmed Minutemen from their silos. Cables were lowered from a transporter/erector truck and attached to the missile by a crew inside the silo. The missile was then slowly raised into the truck and secured for transport.

DEACTIVATION OF THE MINUTEMAN II WEAPON SYSTEM

The fall of the Berlin Wall in November 1989 marked the beginning of the end of the Cold War. On July 31, 1991, President George Bush and Soviet leader Mikhail Gorbachev signed the Strategic Arms Reduction Treaty (START), which placed a limit on the worldwide number of ICBMs and prescribed a process for their destruction. The treaty coincided with the end of the Cold War, and the Air Force's growing disenchantment with the escalating costs of repairing and maintaining the Minuteman II system. On September 27, 1991, President Bush announced on national television his "plan for peace." As part of the plan, Bush called for "the withdrawal from alert, within 72 hours," of all 450 Minuteman II missiles, including those at Ellsworth AFB.

On December 3, 1991, an Air Force crew arrived to remove the first of Ellsworth AFB's 150 Minuteman II missiles: Golf Two (G-2), a launch facility near Red Owl, about 60 miles northeast of Rapid City. The *Rapid City Daily Journal* reported on the crew's progress.

> *Disarmament began with snow shovels at dawn . . . as Airman 1st Class James Comfert and his colleagues cleared the launch-door rail. . . . Six hours later, a Minuteman II intercontinental ballistic missile was stored safely in its transporter/erector truck. G-2 was just a high-tech hole in the ground.*

According to the *Rapid City Daily Journal*, the Minuteman deactivation process at Ellsworth AFB would continue for at least three more years:

> *First, warheads and guidance systems [will be] removed. Then the missiles will be pulled. . . . The headframes of the missile silos will be destroyed and the tubes will be filled with rubble. The launch control capsules will be buried under rubble and a thick concrete cap. The land and above-ground buildings at launch control centers will be sold.*

Although all of the Minuteman II facilities at Ellsworth AFB were slated for demolition, the Air Force, in conjunction with the National Park Service, selected two representative sites — Launch Control Facility Delta One and Launch Facility Delta Nine — for possible preservation as nationally significant icons of the Cold War. When the Minuteman II deactivation is completed in the mid-1990s, these two Ellsworth AFB sites will be the only remaining intact examples of the original Minuteman configuration.

Delta Nine Missile Pull, 1993

1

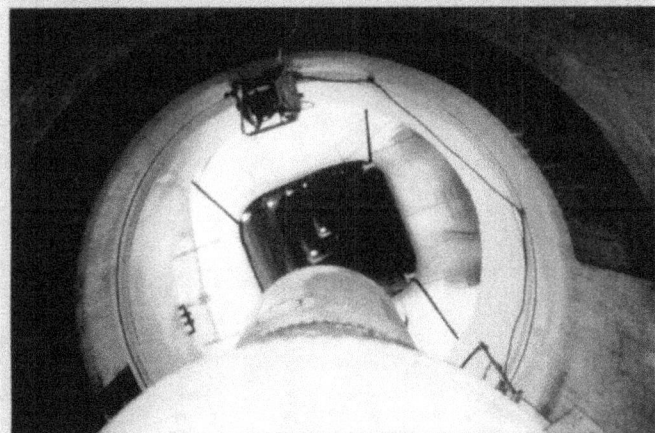

2

3

4

5

6

Site Description

The pastoral setting of the farm and ranch land near Ellsworth AFB belies that area's pivotal role in the Cold War. Beneath the prairie, in an area encompassing 13,500 square miles, were 150 underground missile silos, each equipped with a nuclear-armed Minuteman. Also underground were 15 launch control centers, where Minuteman missileers were on duty 24 hours a day.

The Delta One Launch Control Facility and the Delta Nine Launch Facility survive as excellent examples of this "underground" Air Force. Together, these two facilities could offer visitors the full story of the Minuteman missile system. Visitors would be able to enter an underground launch control center and watch a demonstration of a launch countdown, view a missile silo equipped with a disarmed Minuteman II missile, tour the support facilities and see how Air Force personnel lived in the missile field, and learn about the myriad safety and security measures taken to protect an ICBM site.

DELTA ONE

Site Description

The Delta One Launch Control Facility occupies an open, grassy 6.35-acre tract of land on the west side of Jackson County Road CS 23A, approximately 1.7 miles north of Interstate 90 at Exit 127. A barbed-wire security fence encloses Delta One. Access is controlled through a remote-controlled, chain-link, sliding gate.

Launch Control Facility (LCF) Support Building

Located just inside the sliding gate, the LCF support building provided lodging and cooking facilities for Air Force personnel, served as the security control center for Delta Flight, and housed environmental and electrical systems equipment for the underground launch control center. Prior to the 1993 deactivation of Delta One, a ten-person crew continuously staffed the LCF. Two officers stood vigil in the underground launch control center, replaced each morning by a new missile combat crew dispatched from Ellsworth AFB. Eight topside support personnel, including two flight security controllers, two two-person armed response teams, a cook, and a facility manager, worked three-day shifts.

The support building's main entrance is on the south side. The door opens into a narrow hallway that leads to a spacious dayroom that personnel used during their off-time to read, watch television, and relax. A kitchen and

---

Left: *Delta One's setting is typical of South Dakota's rolling, pastoral land — used for both farming and ranching.* ROBERT LYON

The entrance to Delta One is locked. In the event that Delta One becomes part of a Minuteman Missile National Historic Site, access would be controlled. Visitors would enter the site via shuttle buses, perhaps in military transport vehicles similar to those used by Ellsworth AFB personnel.

From within the security control center at Delta One, guards controlled access to the site, checked visitors' credentials, and monitored radio transmissions. The police also monitored the security of the ten unmanned Delta Flight missile silos. Microwave detection systems and seismic sensors could detect any disturbances at a launch facility. If alarms indicated a disturbance, the guards would dispatch an armored Peacekeeper vehicle to investigate **(below).**

small dining area adjoin the dayroom to the west. A doorway at the west end of the room opens into a long central hallway flanked by seven bedrooms, men's and women's restrooms, and a utility room.

A doorway on the east side of the main entrance hall opens directly into the security control center. This room served as headquarters for the security police who constantly monitored Delta Flight. From a console in this room, guards observed the main entrance, operated the gate, checked visitors' credentials, and monitored radio transmissions. When alarms indicated that a missile silo area may have been breached, the guards also dispatched and monitored the armed response teams.

Launch Control Center (LCC)

The Delta One LCC is 31 feet beneath the support building. This blast-hardened structure served as the command post for the ten dispersed missiles of Delta Flight. After going

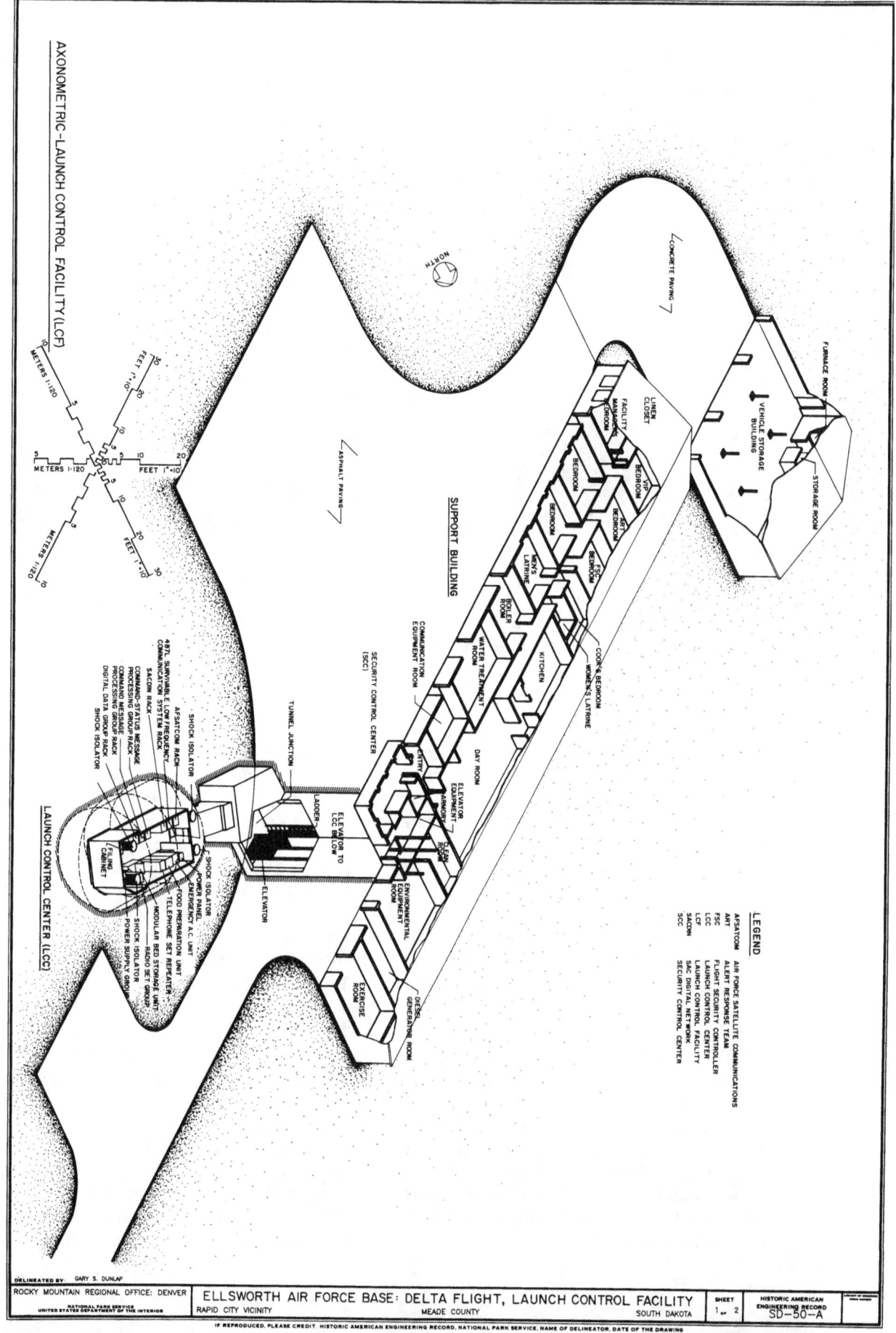

MINUTEMAN SPECIAL RESOURCE STUDY

Delta One's LCF support building provided eating and sleeping facilities for Air Force personnel, and had bedrooms, a kitchen and dining room, and a dayroom. Crew members spent their off hours reading, watching television, and relaxing.

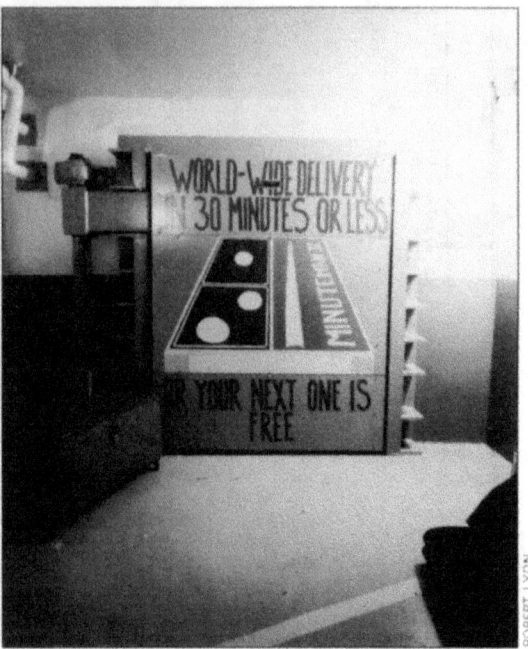

Like the crews who painted "nose art" on military aircraft during World War II, the Cold War's missileers often decorated the blast doors of underground LCCs.

through security clearance, Delta One launch control officers entered the LCC via an elevator. A short corridor leads from the elevator to the launch control center. A sign on the wall and a yellow line painted across the floor mark the beginning of the LCC's ultra-high-security, "no-lone zone." Anyone crossing that line had to be accompanied or observed by another person who could detect erratic behavior or sabotage attempts. Launch control officers carried sidearms and were authorized to shoot in order to guard against sabotage or an unauthorized launch.

The entrance to the underground LCC capsule is sealed by an eight-ton, blast-proof, steel-and-concrete door. Artwork on the door serves as a darkly humorous reminder of the LCC's ultimate purpose. Emblazoned on the door's outer face is a painted depiction of a red, white, and blue pizza delivery box labeled "Minuteman II." A hand-lettered legend reads: "World-wide delivery in 30 minutes or less, or your next one is free."

The LCC is a protective shell, shaped like an enormous capsule. The shell measures 29 feet in diameter and 54 feet in length (outside dimensions), and is constructed of heavily reinforced concrete with four-foot-thick walls. The interior surface is lined with 1/4-inch-thick steel plate. Suspended inside the shell is a box-like acoustical enclosure containing the launch control consoles, communications and missile-monitoring equipment, and accommodations for the two-person launch crew.

The acoustical enclosure is rectangular in plan, measuring approximately 12 feet wide and 28 feet long. Each corner of the room is suspended by a large pneumatic cylinder called a "shock isolator," which would help the control room survive a near-hit from a nuclear weapon. Hanging from heavy chains attached to the ceiling of the shell, the shock isolators would allow the enclosure to bounce in any direction with only minimal damage.

The LCC contains two consoles. Each console has a swiveling, high-backed, aircraft seat

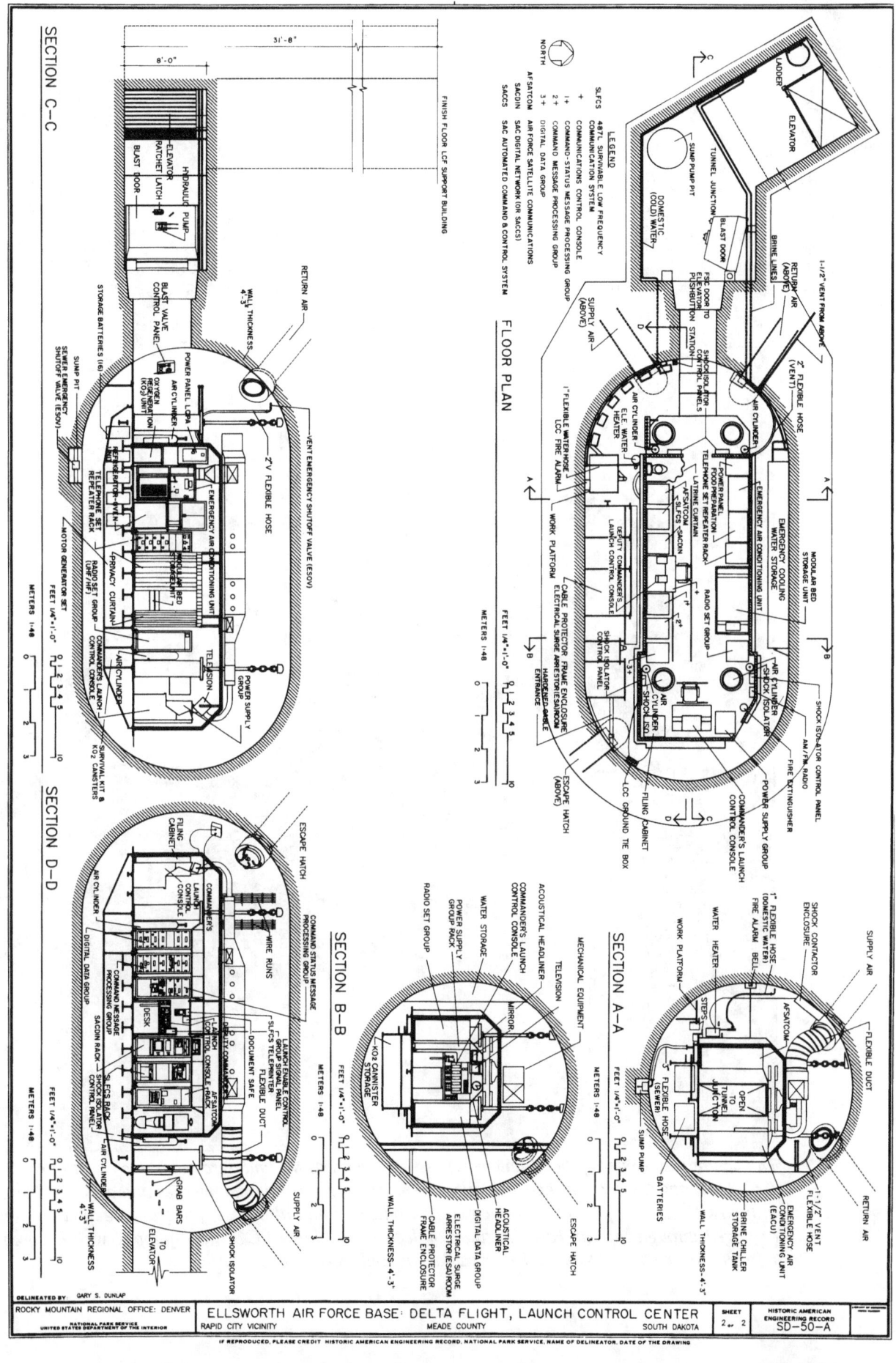

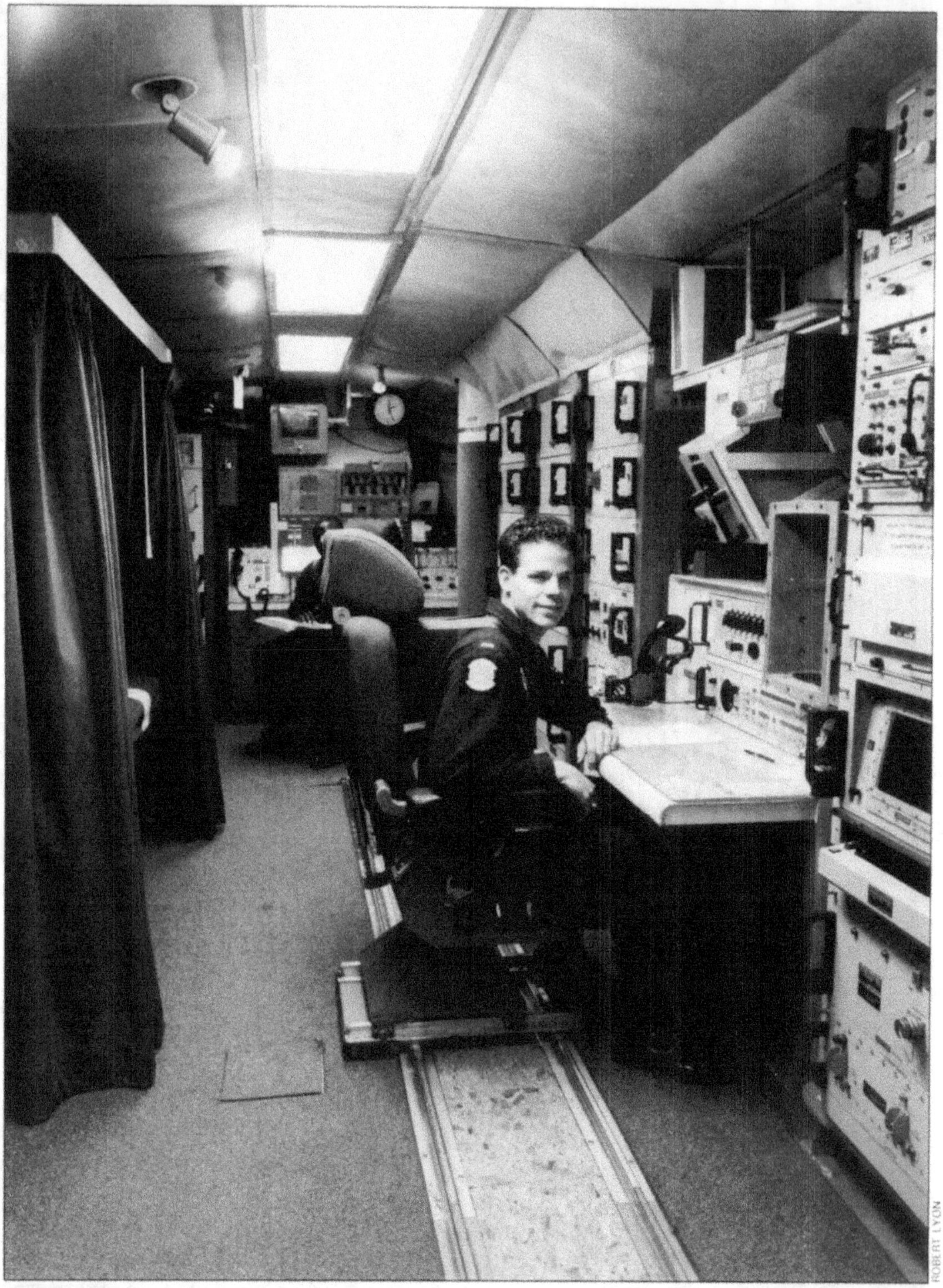

The operational center of the Minuteman missile system was the underground launch control center (LCC). During their round-the-clock duty, the missile crews monitored missiles and conducted tests in the LCC. As time permitted, launch control officers could also study for graduate-level courses arranged through the Air Force Institute of Technology. Each LCC was equipped with an oven, refrigerator, bunk, lavatory, and survival kit, as well as an escape hatch.

> ## Countdown to Doomsday
>
> Only one person could authorize a Minuteman missile launch: the President of the United States. As Commander in Chief of the Armed Services, the President could issue that order in response to an enemy attack. Warning of an attack would come from one of two sources: from early-warning satellites with infra-red sensors that could detect the engine heat of incoming missiles, or from ground-based, coastal radars that could discern submarine-launched missiles. The North American Aerospace Defense Command (NORAD) would then inform the President, who could execute the appropriate response.
>
> In the Delta One LCC, an alarm would have alerted the two-person missile crew of those directives. Immediately, over the speaker system, the launch control officers would hear a coded message, giving the command to launch. After verifying the message's authenticity, the launch officers would unlock a small, red, "Emergency War Order" safe above the deputy commander's control panel. Within the box were two launch keys. Each officer would take one key, and insert it into his or her control console. The missileers would then strap themselves into their console chairs and begin the final countdown. As the commanding officer called out the alphanumeric codes, the deputy commander would verify and repeat the message: "Bravo"... "Bravo"... "Alpha"... "Alpha"... "Lima"... "Lima"...
>
> At the end of the countdown sequence, the officers would turn their launch keys. The Air Force employed several fail-safes to prevent an unauthorized missile launch. For example, both officers had to turn their launch keys in unison. Because the launch switches were 12 feet apart, it was impossible for one person to turn both keys at once. The final command to launch also required another "vote" from outside of Delta One — from either another LCC, or from an airborne command center.
>
> When the second vote came in, the LAUNCH IN PROCESS display would illuminate. Explosive gas generators would then push open the 80-ton launch doors covering the ten Delta Flight missile silos, and the nuclear-tipped Minutemen would begin streaking toward their targets half a world away. As each missile blasted from its silo, its upper umbilical cable would sever, triggering the MISSILE AWAY light on the commander's control panel.
>
> In less than five minutes, the Delta One missileers would have completed their mission. The Minuteman missiles would take another half hour to reach their targets.

fitted with seat belts and a shoulder harness. The LCC's "commander" console is at the east end, directly opposite the entrance. The instrument panel allowed the commander to continually monitor the operational and security status of each of the ten missiles and launchers in Delta Flight. The communications control or "deputy commander" console contains radio, telephone, and decoding equipment that enabled communication with other LCFs, base headquarters, and the Strategic Air Command.

Each of the two consoles includes a small panel that contained a spring-loaded, key-operated launch switch. The launch keys were kept in a red, padlocked, steel box mounted above the deputy commander's console. The walls of the LCC are lined with cabinets filled with computer equipment, radio transmitters and receivers, a telephone relay system, and a power control panel. The LCC is also equipped with a latrine, a small refrigerator and microwave oven unit, and a curtained sleeping compartment.

The LCC ordinarily used commercial electrical power to run its motor-generator, and was provided clean and cooled air from air-conditioning equipment located in the support building. However, the LCC could operate for

The commander's launch control console, which is opposite the entrance of the LCC, tracked the alert status of each of Delta Flight's ten nuclear missiles.

The walls of the Delta One LCC are lined with equipment, including this Command Status Message Processing Group, which is on the south wall.

sustained periods without topside support. In the event of a nuclear attack, an automatic blast valve system would have sealed the capsule off from the surface. The LCC crew could then activate a hand-pumped oxygen regeneration unit. Storage batteries provided emergency electrical power, and an emergency air-conditioning unit would have prevented vital electronic equipment from overheating.

Launch control officers trapped in the LCC after an attack could reach the surface through an escape tube that angles upward from the east end of the capsule. The Air Force plugged the tube at its lower end, and filled it with sand to prevent collapse. To exit, crew members had to remove the plug, dig out the sand, and climb through the tube to the surface.

Vehicle Storage Building

The vehicle storage building is near the northwest corner of the LCF support building. Built in 1968, this structure provided a heated parking area for vehicles, including the front-end loader used for snow removal.

Antennas

Dispersed across the grassy compound on the south side of the support building are two hardened high-frequency (HF) antennas and one ultra-high-frequency (UHF) antenna, which could provide the LCC with an uninterrupted communications link during a nuclear attack. Buried in the ground was a Survivable Low Frequency Communication System antenna.

Sewage Lagoons

Two large sewage lagoons are just outside the security fence, approximately 240 feet southeast of the support building.

Helicopter Pad

Helicopters often transported personnel and equipment between the LCF and the main base at Ellsworth AFB. A large helicopter pad located outside the security fence south of the support building provided a safe landing area.

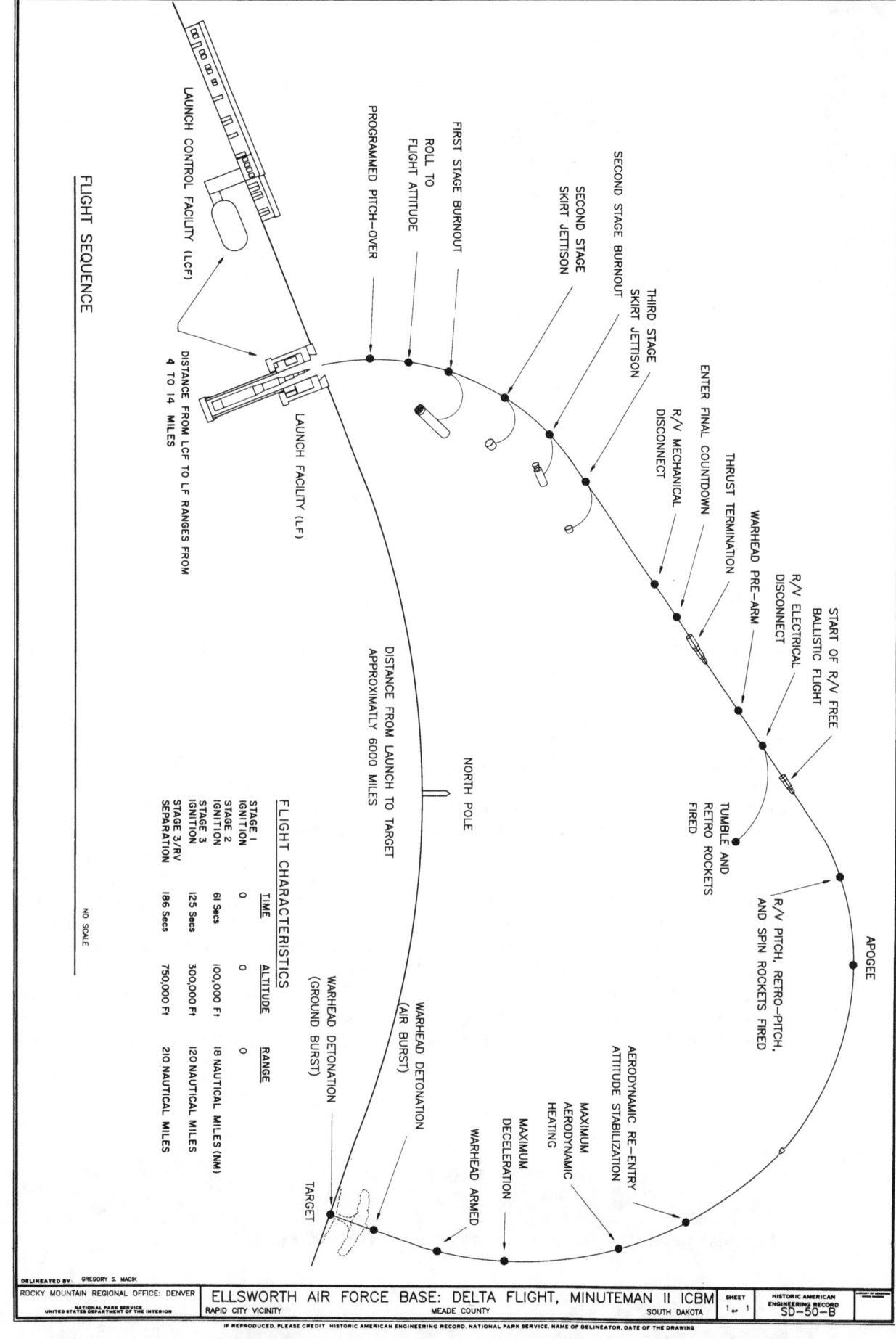

Each LCC was equipped with an escape hatch that led to the surface.

If the Hardened HF Receiving Antenna was damaged during a nuclear strike, a replacement monopole could be quickly raised.

DELTA NINE

Site Description

The Delta Nine Launch Facility is approximately 11 miles west-northwest of Delta One. The launch facility occupies part of an open, grassy, 1.58-acre tract of land along Pennington County Road T512, 0.6 miles west and south of Interstate 90 Exit 116. The tract is roughly rectangular in plan and surrounded by a chain-link security fence with a double gate on the east side. A gravel access drive leads from the nearby county road to the gate.

The Air Force graded the area inside the enclosure to form a level, earthen platform that is elevated a few feet above the surrounding terrain. The platform, which has a gravel surface, provided maneuver space for the transporter-erector vehicles that hauled and emplaced the Minuteman missiles. A smaller rectangular area at the north end of the platform served as a helicopter pad. Flood lights illuminated the area for nighttime maintenance activities.

Missile Launcher

The missile launcher served as a temperature-and-humidity-controlled, long-term storage container, protective enclosure, support facility, and launch pad for a Minuteman missile. The launcher consists of an underground launch tube surrounded by two cylindrical equipment rooms, and covered by a hardened, ballistically-actuated closure door. Air Force personnel could enter the launcher through a heavily-secured hatchway connected to the equipment room.

The launch tube is a reinforced concrete cylinder, lined with 1/4-inch steel plate, 12 feet in diameter (inside dimension), and approxi-

Delta Nine viewed from the access road just off Interstate 90 Exit 116.

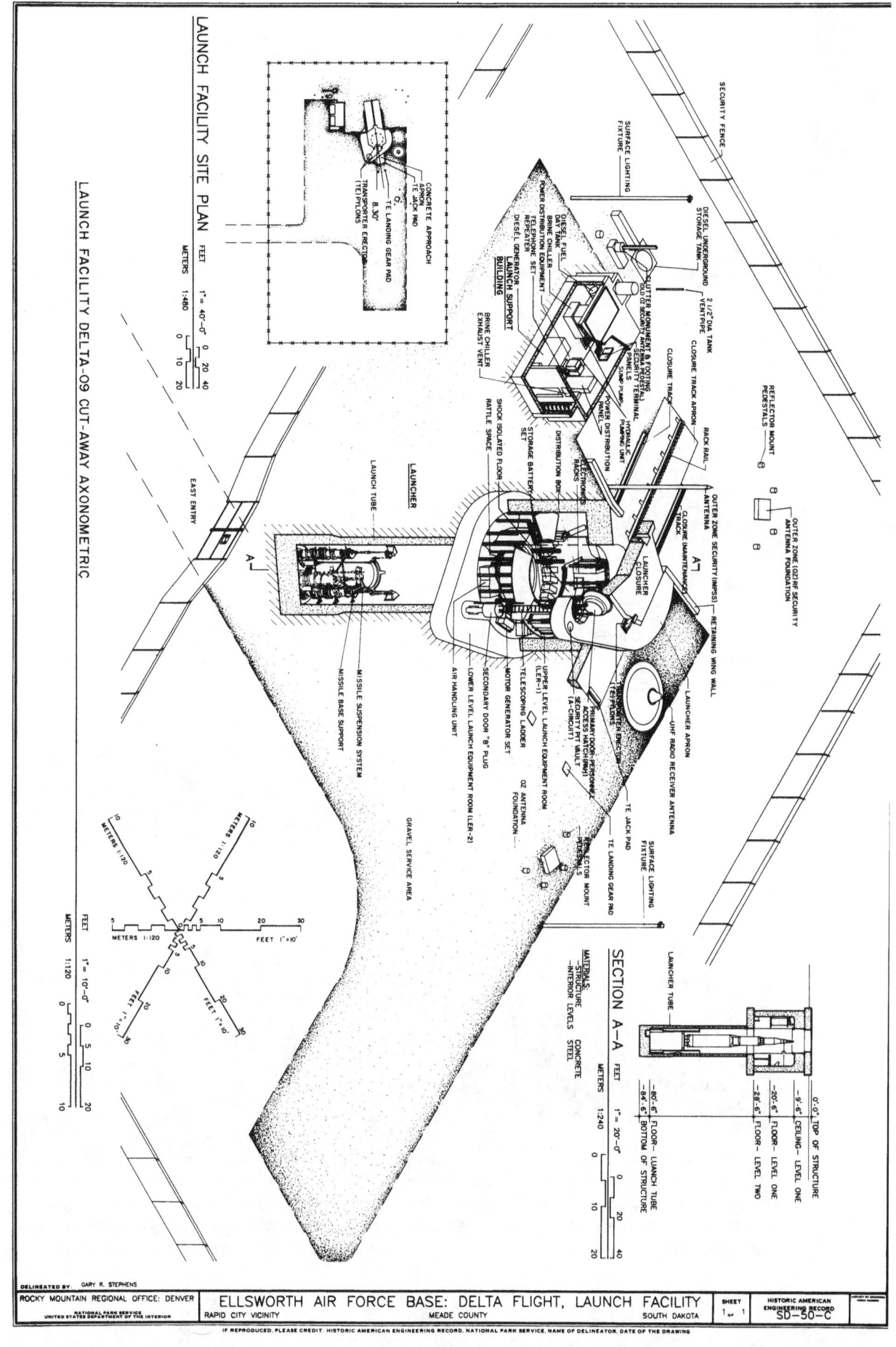

An 80-ton, sliding, reinforced-concrete, closure door covered the silo. Upon receiving the order to launch, explosive gas generators would have quickly pushed the door open.

The personnel hatch at Delta Nine provides access to the missile silo and below-ground equipment rooms.

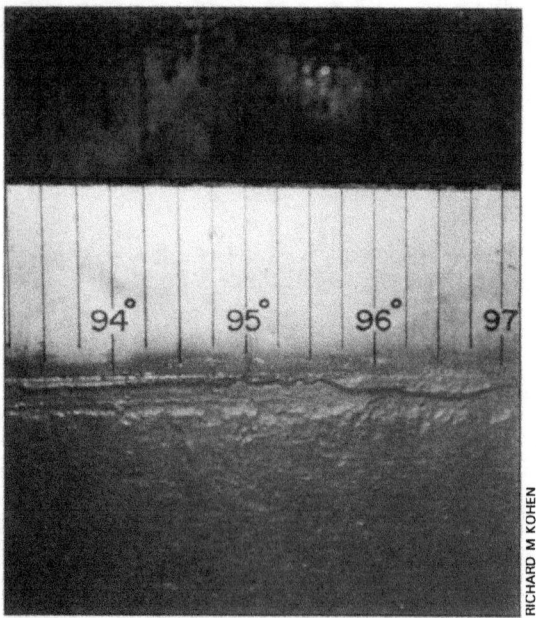

This steel-faced bench, which is calibrated with compass bearings, supported the autocollimator, a complex optical alignment system that was part of Minuteman's guidance system.

mately 80 feet deep. An electrical surge arrestor room is on the southeast exterior wall of the tube's lower level. The surge arrestors would have prevented the electronic equipment inside the launcher from being damaged by the electromagnetic pulse waves of a nuclear explosion. The west half of the lower level contains electrical equipment, including a dozen large emergency batteries. On the outer wall of the upper level is a narrow, steel-faced bench, calibrated with compass bearings. Part of a complex optical alignment system, the bench was the support for an autocollimator, which was used to align the Minuteman missile's guidance system. A porthole or "sight tube" that looked up through the open access hatch was also part of the system. Along the northwest side of the upper level are racks of electronic equipment used to monitor and troubleshoot the missile system, communicate with the LCC, and conduct the countdown.

A massive, reinforced-concrete roof slab covers the launch tube. Cast into the southern edge of the roof slab is a pocket-like opening for the launcher closure door. The hexagonal-shaped, reinforced-concrete, closure door is three and one-half feet thick and weighs more than 80 tons. Prior to launch, a ballistic actuator would have opened the door. If the missile or one of its major components had to be removed or replaced, maintenance workers used a cogged rail in the middle of the track apron to slowly jack the door open.

A white, fiberglass, monopole antenna rises from the base of the roof slab on the east side of the closure-door opening. This antenna is part of a microprocessor-based surveillance system designed to detect intruders at the launch site.

Launch Facility Support Building

Adjacent to the launcher is the underground launch facility support building, which provided electrical power to the site, as well as chilled "brine" to the launcher equipment room air handler. The air handler provided the electronics racks and launcher with temperature-and-humidity-controlled air. The support building contains a diesel-fueled standby power generator, electrical switch gear, a brine chiller, a hydraulic pump for the launcher's personnel access hatch, a temperature-control air compressor, and various panels for mechanical, security, and communications systems.

Antenna

The site's hardened UHF receiving antenna is a few feet northwest of the silo opening. The antenna linked Delta Nine with the Strategic Air Command's airborne launch control center.

Azimuth Markers

The azimuth markers are surveyors' benchmarks that were used in conjunction with the autocollimator to align the Minuteman missile guidance system. Delta Nine has two azimuth markers. One is approximately 1,000 feet northwest of the launcher; the other is approximately 1,000 feet to the north-northeast.

Description of Management Alternatives

COMMON ELEMENTS

The Minuteman Special Resource Study Team developed three management alternatives for Delta One and Delta Nine. These alternatives share three common elements:

- *The 44th Missile Wing has been inactivated. As a result, the US Air Force Museum in Dayton, Ohio, and the 28 Civil Engineers Squadron at Ellsworth AFB are now responsible for the Minuteman equipment and real property at Delta One and Delta Nine. Any organization that acquires Delta One and Delta Nine must negotiate with the Air Force Museum regarding the long-term loan of Minuteman equipment. The Air Force Museum restricts the loan of these items to qualified non-profit organizations or government agencies that agree to make Delta One and Delta Nine open for public visitation (10 USC 2572). This requirement precludes the possibility of Delta One and Delta Nine being developed as a for-profit enterprise.*

- *Under each management alternative, the South Dakota Air and Space Museum, which is located at Ellsworth AFB, would continue its existing Minuteman missile displays. The South Dakota Air and Space Museum, which is an Air Force Museum Program institution, focuses on the history of aviation in South Dakota, including the history of the 44th Missile Wing.*

- *The South Dakota Air and Space Museum has declined the acquisition of Delta One and Delta Nine.*

Left: *A Delta Flight missile being removed from its silo.* ROBERT LYON

ALTERNATIVE 1
No Action

CONCEPT

Under Alternative 1, there would be no acquisition nor preservation of Delta One and Delta Nine. The Air Force would deactivate and demolish Delta One and Delta Nine, as is currently underway with the other Minuteman sites associated with the 44th Missile Wing.

IMPACT ANALYSIS

Delta One and Delta Nine

Under this alternative, the Air Force would dispose of Delta One and Delta Nine as proposed in the *Final Environmental Impact Statement, Deactivation of the Minuteman II Wing at Ellsworth Air Force Base (1991)*.

At Delta Nine, the Air Force would remove the missile and other critical classified items, including reusable equipment. Hazardous materials and underground fuel storage tanks would be properly removed. The Air Force would then demolish the headworks of the missile silo, fill the launch tube with rubble, seal the tube with a below-ground concrete cap, and level and grade the site. The Delta Nine Site would then be offered for sale, first to adjacent landowners, then to other interested parties.

The Air Force would deactivate Delta One in a similar manner. The Air Force would disable the underground launch control center by welding shut the access door, removing the elevator, filling the shaft with rubble, sealing it with concrete, and capping it to deny future access. Although the equipment would be removed, the above-ground facility structures would remain largely intact, and would be offered for sale.

Interpretive Themes

Under all of the management alternatives, the South Dakota Air and Space Museum would continue its exhibits on Minuteman II's presence in South Dakota. These displays focus on the technology of the ICBM weapon system, and its role in the history of aviation in South Dakota.

Visitor Facilities and Services

Although there would be no public visitation to the Delta One and Delta Nine sites, visitors to the South Dakota Air and Space Museum would be able to view a training facsimile of a launch control center that includes a demonstration of a launch sequence. On the grounds surrounding the museum, visitors can see a Minuteman II missile and a missile transporter-erector vehicle. The South Dakota Air and Space Museum also conducts a bus tour of Ellsworth AFB that includes a stop at a Minuteman missile training silo.

Access

There would be no public access to the Delta One and Delta Nine sites.

Training and Employment

No new training nor employment opportunities would result from this alternative.

Acquisition, Development, and Operating Costs

Under this proposal, there would be no acquisition, development, nor operating costs regarding Delta One and Delta Nine.

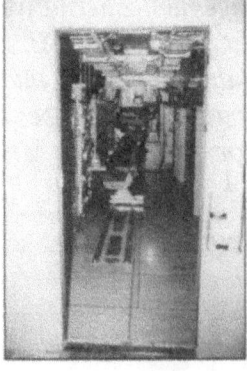

Minuteman launch control officers received training in an LCC facsimile, which was located in a hangar at Ellsworth AFB. The trainer is now located in the South Dakota Air and Space Museum.

Economic Impacts

The Air Force would sell the Delta One and Delta Nine sites. Presumably, the land and surface improvements would revert to agricultural use. Because of the limited acreage involved, the economic impacts would be negligible.

Natural Resources

The US Forest Service property surrounding Delta Nine, in the role of a multi-use area, would continue to be used for grazing. If the land reverts to agricultural use (private or USFS), existing practices affecting the grassland and wetland habitats would continue.

ALTERNATIVE 2

An Organization other than the National Park Service Preserves Delta One and Delta Nine

CONCEPT

Under Alternative 2, a qualified non-profit organization or government agency — but not the National Park Service — would acquire Delta One and Delta Nine and make them available for public visitation, similar to the Titan Missile Museum near Tucson, Arizona. However, despite widespread publicity about the project, no qualified government or non-profit organization has expressed any interest in acquiring these sites.

IMPACT ANALYSIS

Delta One and Delta Nine

Under this alternative, the new owner would acquire Delta One and Delta Nine from the Air Force. The new owner would coordinate with the Air Force Museum regarding the long-term loan of the Minuteman equipment associated with the missile sites. The Air Force Museum will only loan such equipment to qualified non-profits or governments that demonstrate the capability of properly maintaining those artifacts and making them available for public visitation.

Interpretive Themes

The interpretive themes would be the responsibility of the new owner of Delta One and Delta Nine.

Visitor Facilities and Services

The new owner would be responsible for visitor facilities and services. The facilities must meet Air Force Museum requirements regarding curation and public visitation.

Access

Under this alternative, Delta One and Delta Nine would be accessible to the public. The new owner would be responsible for providing that access.

Training and Employment

The new owner would be responsible for training and employment.

Acquisition, Development, and Operating Costs

The new owner would need to negotiate with the Air Force regarding the real property transfer of Delta One and Delta Nine, and would be responsible for any additional development or operating costs.

Economic Impacts

The preservation of Delta One and Delta Nine would have an economic impact in the area as a result of tourist visitation and the additional time that travelers would spend in western Jackson and eastern Pennington Counties. However, since visitation is influenced by visitor facilities, services, and interpretation — as well as by marketing strategy — it is not possible to determine the extent of the economic impacts under this alternative.

Natural Resources

The impact on natural resources is dependent on the actions of the new owner, and the location of any new facilities. No endangered species are in the areas adjacent to Delta One and Delta Nine.

ALTERNATIVE 3
Delta One and Delta Nine as a National Historic Site

CONCEPT

Under Alternative 3, the National Park Service, in conjunction with the Air Force Museum, would acquire, preserve, and interpret Delta One and Delta Nine as a National Historic Site. The site would commemorate the history and significance of the Cold War, the arms race, and ICBM development.

IMPACT ANALYSIS

Delta One and Delta Nine

Under this alternative, the Air Force would deactivate and operationally disable the Delta One and Delta Nine Minuteman facilities. However, the National Park Service, in conjunction with the Air Force and the Air Force Museum, would preserve the historic appearance and viewshed of Delta One and Delta Nine. Also preserved would be the sites' historic furnishings and equipment, including a disarmed Minuteman missile.

Interpretive Themes

The National Park Service would develop an interpretive program for Delta One and Delta Nine that would focus on: 1) the larger political, philosophical, diplomatic, and societal issues of the Cold War; 2) the human aspects of military training and readiness; and 3) ICBM technology. The National Park Service would encourage visitors to determine for themselves the most important lessons of the Cold War, including the global implications of missile deployment. Capitalizing on virtually every visitor's own experiences, site interpretation would touch individual memories and emotional responses to the Cold War.

Integral to the interpretation is the preservation of the operational character of Delta One and Delta Nine. As such, there would be no adaptive reuse of either facility, and the National Park Service would maintain the historic appearance of Delta One and Delta Nine. Visitors to Delta One would feel that they were viewing a "day in the life" of a Minuteman missile crew. The interpretation would also impart a sense of the US military's commitment to the mission of maintaining world peace.

Under this alternative, both the Minuteman Missile National Historic Site and the South Dakota Air and Space Museum would have interpretive programs. However, these programs would not be duplicative; each would reflect different aspects of the Minuteman weapon system. The National Park Service would develop an interpretive program that complements that of the South Dakota Air and Space Museum — offering visitors the full story of the ICBM system within the broader context of the Cold War.

Visitor Facilities and Services

Minuteman Missile National Historic Site facilities would include Delta One, Delta Nine, and a visitor center. Following are preliminary concepts:

Visitor Center. In order to preserve the historic character of Delta One and Delta Nine, the Minuteman Missile National Historic Site Visitor Center would be located off-site from the missile facilities. At the visitor center, the National Park Service would provide an opportunity for visitors to prepare intellectually and emotionally for the experience of visiting Delta One, which would be preserved as a virtually intact launch control facility. The visitor center would have a physical staging area to move visitors to Delta One. The center would also include an exhibit area, administrative offices, an auditorium, rest rooms, a research library, a gift shop, a parking area, and shuttle bus loading/unloading facilities. The visitor center's operational facilities would include a small maintenance yard, and also may include employee housing.

Delta One. Visitors would only be able to see Delta One as part of a guided tour, and would need to make tour arrangements at the Minuteman Missile National Historic Site Visitor Center. Delta One includes the underground LCC, where visitors would be able to see the actual equipment and turn-key procedures used to launch Minuteman missiles. The aboveground buildings include sleeping, eating, and

Property Ownership

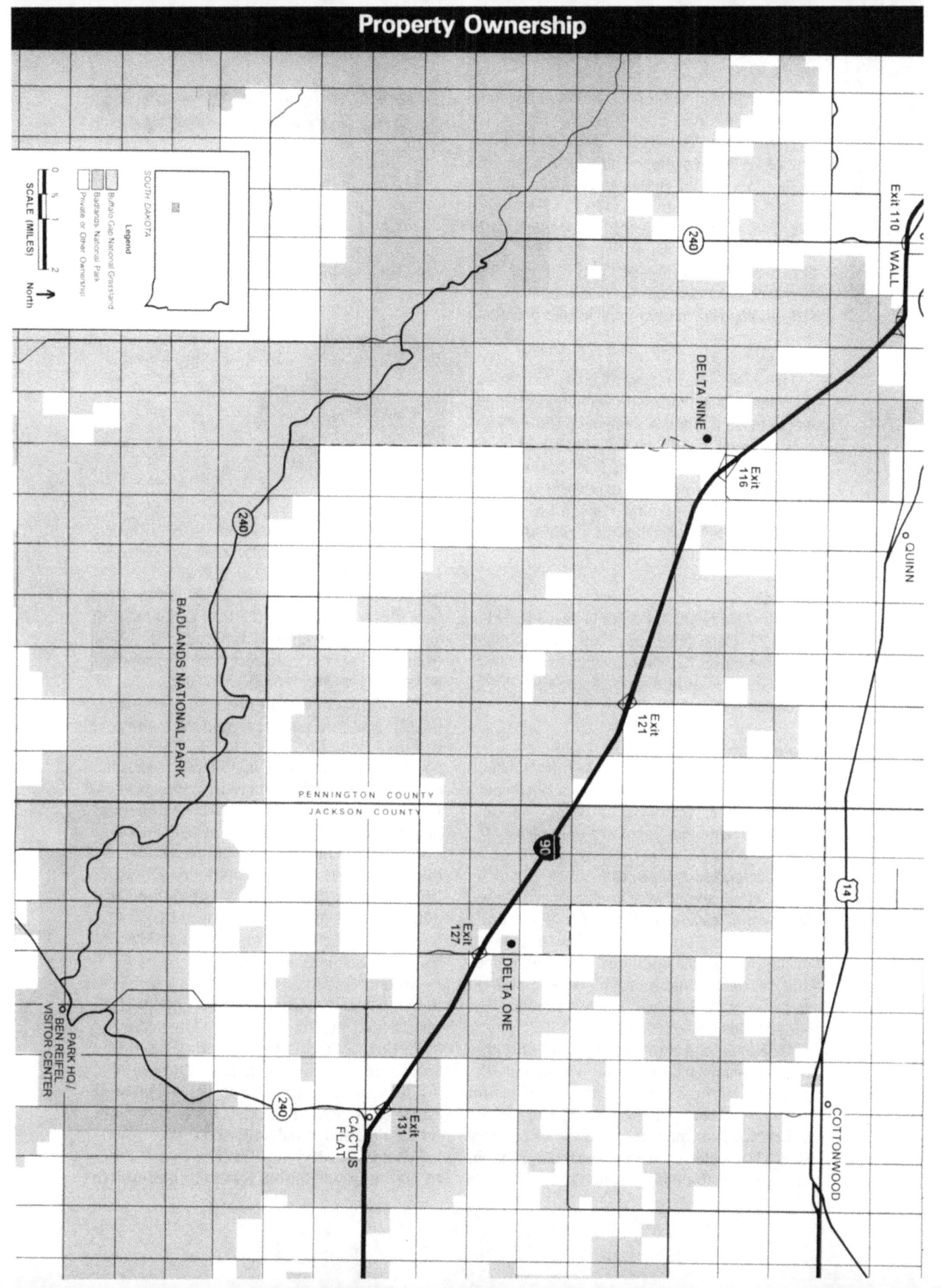

recreational facilities for the missile crew, and would be preserved in their existing state.

Delta Nine. Visitors could see Delta Nine, one of ten missile silos controlled remotely by Delta One, on self-guided tours. Delta Nine is located 11 miles from Delta One. A clear cover over the missile silo would allow visitors to peer down into the launch tube and see a disarmed Minuteman missile. The National Park Service would develop wayside exhibits and a self-guiding brochure to provide interpretation.

Zoning

Delta One is in Jackson County, which has no zoning. Delta Nine is in Pennington County, where the agricultural zoning allows for a wide range of uses. To protect the character of the missile sites, the National Park Service may need to acquire scenic easements or land trades. Outright purchase of land to protect the scenic resources, however, would not be pursued.

Access

Delta One is located north of Interstate 90 at Exit 127. Delta Nine is at Exit 116. Although the location of the visitor center has not been finalized, it would also be accessible off of Interstate 90.

Training and Employment

To staff the Minuteman Missile National Historic Site, the National Park Service could recruit former 44th Missile Wing personnel who have retired and now live in the area.

Socioeconomic Impacts

The Minuteman Missile National Historic Site would have significant socioeconomic impacts in the area as a result of increased visitation, and the additional time and money that travelers would spend in western Jackson and eastern Pennington Counties and the Pine Ridge Indian Reservation.

However, the impacts of the Minuteman Missile National Historic Site would vary depending on the location and type of visitor center. Preliminary studies indicate that either a stand-alone or multi-resource visitor center at Exit 131 would receive the greatest visitation, primarily because of its location at the interstate

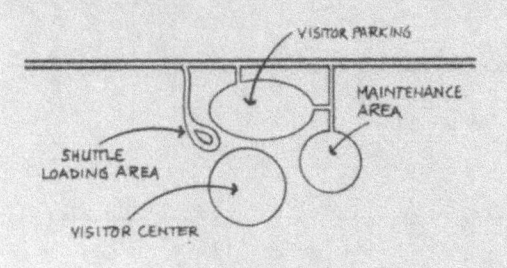

Visitor Center Conceptual Plan

Under Alternative 3, the Minuteman Missile National Historic Site Visitor Center would be located off Interstate 90. The center would include an exhibit area, offices, visitor parking, maintenance yard, and shuttle loading area.

exit to Badlands National Park. It is estimated that a multi-resource visitor center at Exit 131 would attract between 231,000 and 315,000 people during the first year of operation. Five years later, between 307,000 and 418,000 annual visitors would be expected. Ten years from opening, the visitation would be approximately 409,000 to 556,000 annually.

Based on a midpoint projection, approximately 362,500 people would visit a multi-resource center at Exit 131 five years after opening. However, it is important to note that only about 45% of this number represents *new* visitors — an *incremental* increase above and beyond the normal visitation at Badlands National Park. On average, people who would stop at the visitor center would spend an extra half day in the area. Thus, it is estimated that a multi-resource visitor center at Exit 131 would generate approximately 163,000 *new* half-day visitations per year.

An estimated 163,000 half-day visitations to the area every year would result in approximately $3.2 million dollars of additional travel spending. This visitor spending would be associated with approximately 126 new jobs, which would be located in the vicinity of Badlands National Park, and various locations on the Pine Ridge Indian Reservation.

A stand-alone visitor center at Exit 127, although more desirable from an interpretive

Delta Nine Conceptual Improvements Plan

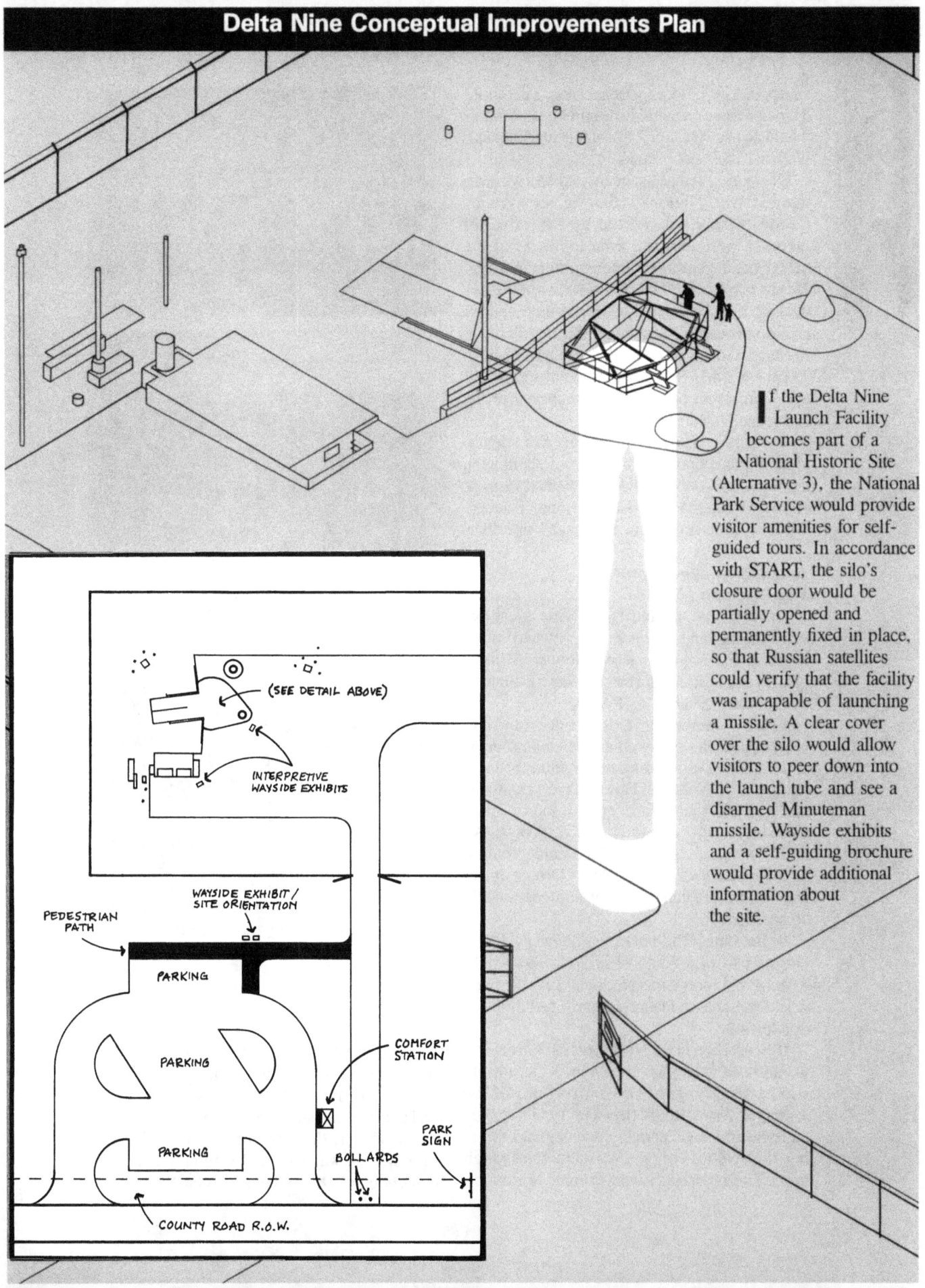

If the Delta Nine Launch Facility becomes part of a National Historic Site (Alternative 3), the National Park Service would provide visitor amenities for self-guided tours. In accordance with START, the silo's closure door would be partially opened and permanently fixed in place, so that Russian satellites could verify that the facility was incapable of launching a missile. A clear cover over the silo would allow visitors to peer down into the launch tube and see a disarmed Minuteman missile. Wayside exhibits and a self-guiding brochure would provide additional information about the site.

standpoint, would experience less visitation. This is because a significant number of visitors would bypass Exit 127 by taking the Badlands National Park Loop Road.

Of course, actual attendance to the Minuteman Missile National Historic Site Visitor Center would be affected by a number of factors, including the final location of the center, management structure, and marketing. Demographic and socioeconomic profiles indicate that a strong cross-marketing strategy could successfully persuade the majority of Minuteman visitors to also visit the South Dakota Air and Space Museum, which would give tourists an opportunity to experience the full range of available resources.

For a more detailed discussion of the demographic and economic conditions of Pennington and Jackson Counties and the potential impacts of the Minuteman Missile National Historic Site, see "Socioeconomic Analysis," page 83.

Acquisition, Development, and Operating Costs

Since Delta One and Delta Nine and most surrounding lands are Federally-owned, there would be no acquisition costs for the Minuteman Missile National Historic Site. Estimated development costs are as follows:

Visitor Center. Development costs would vary, depending on whether the visitor center is designed as a stand-alone or multi-resource facility. The National Park Service estimates that a 10,000-square-foot, multi-resource center would cost approximately $4,529,800. An 8,000-square-foot, stand-alone center would cost approximately $3,953,800. Design, planning, and construction supervision costs would be additional.

Delta One. The cost of renovating Delta One as part of a National Historic Site would be minimal, since the National Park Service would preserve the launch control facility in its existing state.

Delta Nine. The National Park Service would need to modify the Delta Nine missile silo to comply with the requirements of the Strategic Arms Reduction Treaty. These requirements include partially opening and securing the sliding concrete door of the launch tube. The National Park Service would also

Several exits along Interstate 90 could serve as the location for the Minuteman Missile National Historic Site Visitor Center: **Top:** *Exit 121 is midway between Delta One and Delta Nine.* **Center:** *Exit 127 is the closest to Delta One.* **Bottom:** *Exit 131 leads south to Badlands National Park. Federal land is available at all of these exits.*

construct visitor facilities at Delta Nine, including viewing platforms, a parking lot, restrooms, walkways, and lighting. These costs are estimated at $323,365. Design, planning, and construction supervision would be additional. However, the Air Force may reallocate money that was originally intended for the demolition of Delta One and Delta Nine for the conversion of Delta Nine into a static display.

Thus, the cost of a multi-resource visitor center, together with improvements at Delta One and Delta Nine, would be approximately $4,853,165. A stand-alone center, including improvements at Delta One and Delta Nine, would cost approximately $4,277,165. (As noted above, these estimates do not include design, planning, and construction supervision.) Prior to building any new facilities, the National Park Service would conduct archeological and environmental impact surveys of the proposed construction areas.

Estimated operating costs also vary, depending on the administrative relationship between the proposed National Historic Site and Badlands National Park. The National Park Service estimates that eight full-time and four seasonal employees are needed to administer the National Historic Site, which would cost approximately $400,000 to $600,000 annually. However, if the National Park Service establishes the Minuteman Missile National Historic Site as part of Badlands National Park, there would be considerable savings in terms of administration, security, and maintenance.

Fees

The National Park Service would not charge a fee for admission to the visitor center. Delta Nine would be visited as part of a free, self-guided tour. However, visitors would only be able to see Delta One as part of a guided tour. The annual tour capacity of Delta One is approximately 87,000. A tour fee of $3.00 per person — assuming reduced rates for groups, children, and seniors — would generate approximately $125,000-$175,000 annually. Given the limited tour capacity of Delta One, the National Park Service may also need to develop a tour reservation system.

Natural Resources

There are no endangered plant or animal species in the area. However, Delta One, Delta Nine, and all of the possible locations for a visitor center are located in or adjacent to a black-footed ferret experimental reintroduction area. Within this area, ferrets are classified as *experimental* rather than *endangered*. The National Park Service, which is involved in the reintroduction effort, would be careful not to negatively impact the ferrets.

New construction would not be sited in flood plains or wetlands, and no impacts on wetlands are anticipated. A well would supply water for facility development and visitor use, which could affect groundwater supplies. The well at Delta One is 2,965 feet deep and taps the Fall River Aquifer.

OTHER ALTERNATIVES CONSIDERED

The Minuteman Special Resource Study Team evaluated several other management alternatives, including the possibility of corporate acquisition of Delta One and Delta Nine. This option was rejected due to the Air Force Museum's requirement (10 USC 2572) that Minuteman artifacts can be loaned only to qualified non-profit organizations and government agencies. However, a corporate sponsor could provide start-up and/or construction funds.

The team also considered the possibility of preserving Delta One and Delta Nine for research purposes only. Under this alternative, the sites would be "mothballed" but would not be restored nor made available for public visitation. But Air Force Museum restrictions prevent this alternative. The Air Force Museum, which is responsible for historic equipment at Delta One and Delta Nine now that the 44th Missile Wing has been inactivated, will only allow that equipment to remain if the sites are open to the public.

Possible Visitor Center Locations

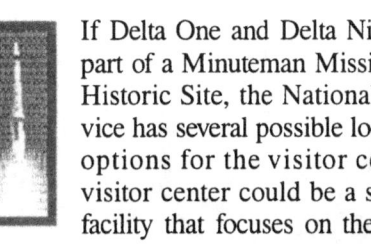

If Delta One and Delta Nine become part of a Minuteman Missile National Historic Site, the National Park Service has several possible locations and options for the visitor center. The visitor center could be a stand-alone facility that focuses on the Cold War and the Minuteman missile system. Or the Minuteman Missile National Historic Site could share a visitor center with other Great Plains attractions — such as Badlands National Park and the Big Foot Trail to Wounded Knee. This multi-resource approach would offer visitors an overview of the rich heritage of the Great Plains — including the geological and paleontological wonders of the badlands, the history of homesteading in the area, Lakota culture, and the role the Great Plains played in America's national defense during the Cold War years.

Possible locations for the Minuteman Missile National Historic Site Visitor Center include:

EXIT 131

A visitor center at Exit 131 received the greatest support from the public. Exit 131 is at the eastern end of Highway 240, the Badlands National Park Loop Road. The exit is four miles east of Delta One.

BADLANDS NATIONAL PARK

The Badlands National Park Visitor Center could be expanded to include administrative and visitor facilities for the Minuteman Missile National Historic Site.

EXIT 127

Closest to Delta One, a visitor center at this exit would provide maximum security for the missile site. The Minuteman Special Resource Study Team evaluated converting Delta One into a visitor center, but discarded that option because it would destroy the facility's historic character and diminish the interpretive experience. However, a new visitor center south of Interstate 90 at Exit 127 would not affect the historic integrity of Delta One.

EXIT 121

Midway between Delta One and Delta Nine, Exit 121 is the closest to Chief Big Foot's Trail

---

Left: *The underground missile silo includes an upper-level equipment room. The launch tube (left side of photo) is encircled by computer and electronic racks, air conditioning units, and other equipment.* RICHARD M. KOHEN

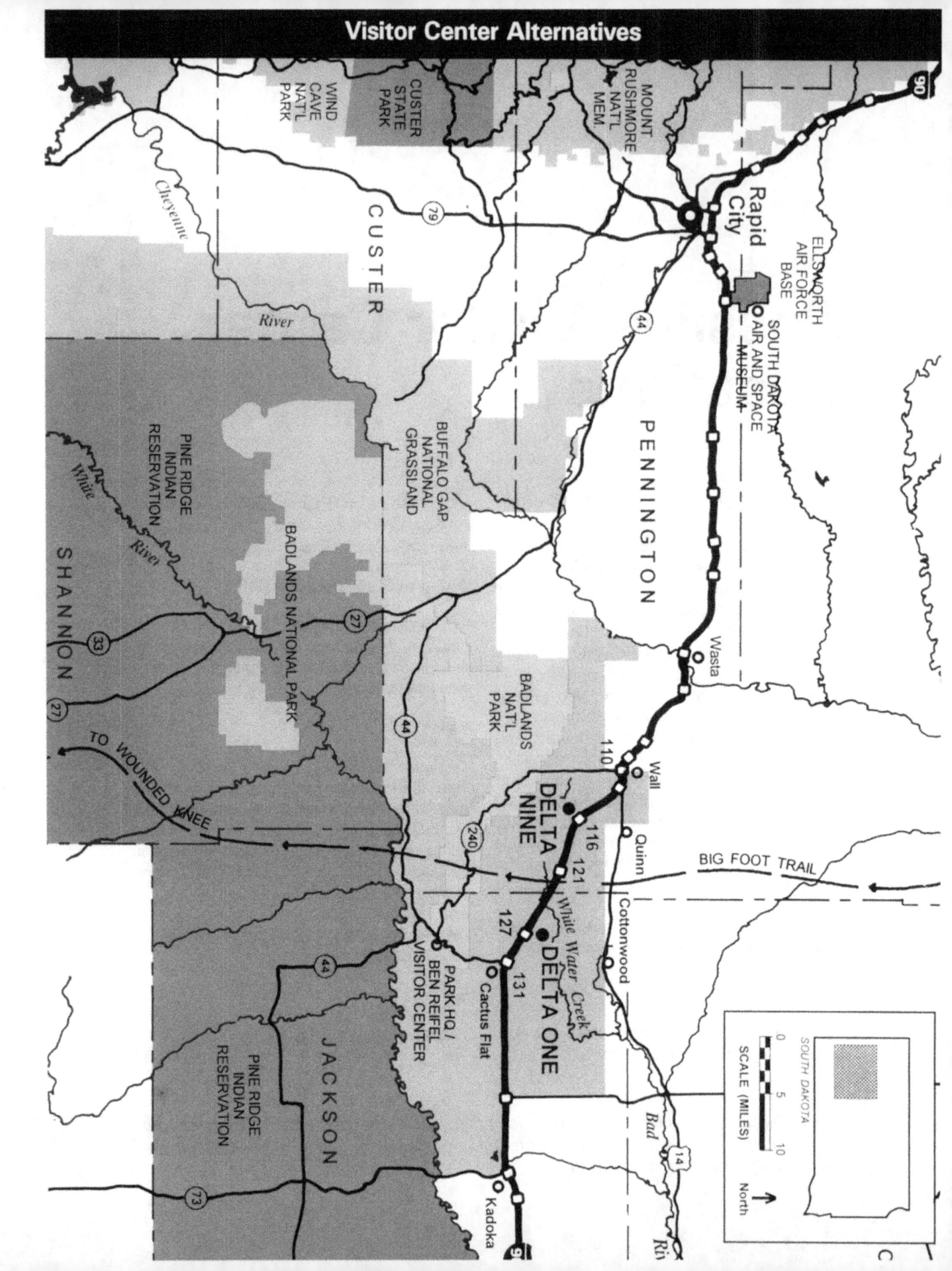

to Wounded Knee. The Lakota Sioux have expressed a desire to have a visitor center off of Interstate 90 that would interpret the journey of Chief Big Foot and his band of Minneconjous Lakota to Wounded Knee.

EXIT 116

This exit is the closest to Delta Nine.

EXIT 110

Located at the town of Wall, Exit 110 is the western end of the Badlands National Park Loop Road. The study team examined the feasibility of integrating the Minuteman Missile Visitor Center into the newly-constructed US Forest Service center in Wall. Although it would combine two Federally-operated visitor facilities, this option received no support from the public.

SOUTH DAKOTA AIR AND SPACE MUSEUM, ELLSWORTH AFB

Visitors could get an initial orientation to the Minuteman missile system at the South Dakota Air and Space Museum, and then take bus tours to Delta One and Delta Nine. Delta One is approximately 70 miles east of the museum.

Popular support for these alternatives is discussed in the "Summary of Public Responses," beginning on page 91. For additional visitor center factors, such as traffic patterns and projected visitation, see "Socioeconomic Analysis," page 83.

◂ BIG FOOT TRAIL TO WOUNDED KNEE

Under Alternative 3, the National Park Service may construct a multi-resource visitor center that could include interpretation of Minuteman, Badlands National Park, and the Big Foot Trail to Wounded Knee. The massacre at Wounded Knee represented a turning point in the history of Indian/White relations and symbolized the end of the traditional Lakota way of life. On December 23, 1890, Chief Big Foot's band of Minneconjous Lakota left their village near the forks of the Cheyenne River and headed south across the badlands towards Pine Ridge Indian Reservation. For five days, they eluded the US Army. But on December 28, the Seventh Cavalry captured the Indians and escorted them to the banks of Wounded Knee Creek. The following morning, fighting erupted — resulting in the deaths of more than 250 Lakota men, women, and children.

MINUTEMAN SPECIAL RESOURCE STUDY

PROS AND CONS OF VISITOR CENTER TYPE AND LOCATION

Under Alternative 3, the National Park Service would administer Delta One and Delta Nine as a Minuteman Missile National Historic Site. The Minuteman Special Resource Study Team analyzed the advantages and disadvantages of a stand-alone versus multi-resource visitor center, as well as possible locations. Following are some *pros* and *cons* of each option:

TYPE OF VISITOR CENTER

Stand-Alone Visitor Center

Pros	Cons
• Optimum visitor experience for the Minuteman Missile National Historic Site. • Approximately $576,000 less to build than a multi-resource center. • Greater ability to recruit staff from local, retired, Air Force personnel.	• Would be difficult to justify another Federal visitor center in proximity to Badlands National Park and the US Forest Service Visitor Center at Wall.

Multi-Resource Visitor Center

Pros	Cons
• Received the most public support. • If located at Exit 131, could relieve pressure on the Badlands National Park Visitor Center during the peak, summer tourist season. • If located at Exit 121, could help satisfy a Lakota desire for a tourist center for Wounded Knee and the Big Foot Trail along Interstate 90. • Lower staffing and maintenance costs. • Cost-effective way to meet visitor needs at Badlands National Park, the Minuteman Missile National Historic Site, and Big Foot Trail/Wounded Knee.	• Dilutes visitor experience for the Minuteman Missile National Historic Site. • Approximately $576,000 more to build than a stand-alone center. • Greater difficulty in hiring interpreters who are knowledgeable about a broad range of subjects, such as paleontology, ecology, Lakota culture, and ICBM missile systems.

PROS AND CONS OF VISITOR CENTER TYPE AND LOCATION

LOCATION OF VISITOR CENTER

Exit 131

Pros
- Received the most public support; strongly endorsed by local business community.
- A multi-resource center at this location would provide westbound travelers with at least three tourist destinations: Big Foot Trail/Wounded Knee, Minuteman, and Badlands National Park.
- Would generate the highest visitation.
- Could relieve pressure on the Badlands National Park Visitor Center during the peak, summer tourist season.
- Proximity of existing tourist services.
- Available Federal land.

Cons
- Dilutes visitor experience for the Minuteman Missile National Historic Site.
- NPS experience has shown that a visitor center located away from the resource tends to be underused and less successful. In the case of Exit 131, a multi-resource visitor center would be located off-site from its three major interpretive themes: Minuteman, Badlands National Park, and Big Foot Trail/Wounded Knee.

Badlands National Park
(This option would add the interpretation and administration of the Minuteman National Historic Site to the existing Badlands National Park Visitor Center.)

Pros
- Least expensive alternative.

Cons
- 20-mile round-trip bus ride to Delta One.
- Dilutes visitor experience for the Minuteman Missile National Historic Site.
- Puts additional strain on the Badlands National Park Visitor Center, as well as the highway leading into the park.
- NPS experience has shown that a visitor center located away from the resource tends to be underused and less successful.
- Additional funding for the Minuteman Missile National Historic Site could be jeopardized if not a separate NPS unit.

PROS AND CONS OF VISITOR CENTER TYPE AND LOCATION

LOCATION OF VISITOR CENTER
Continued

Exit 127

Pros
- Closest to Delta One; shortest bus ride for visitors.
- Better security for Delta One.
- Available Federal land.

Cons
- Any visitor center west of Exit 131 would receive less visitation because it would be bypassed by tourists taking the Badlands National Park Loop Road.

Exit 121

Pros
- Midway between Delta One and Delta Nine.
- Closest exit to the Big Foot Trail.
- Available Federal land.

Cons
- Most visitors would have to backtrack six miles to visit Delta One.
- Any visitor center west of Exit 131 would receive less visitation because it would be bypassed by tourists taking the Badlands National Park Loop Road.
- NPS experience has shown that a visitor center located away from the resource tends to be underused and less successful.

Exit 116

Pros
- Closest exit to Delta Nine.
- Available Federal land.

Cons
- Destroys historic viewshed and sense of isolation of Delta Nine.
- Any visitor center west of Exit 131 would receive less visitation because it would be bypassed by tourists taking the Badlands National Park Loop Road.
- Most visitors would have to backtrack 11 miles to visit Delta One.

PROS AND CONS OF VISITOR CENTER TYPE AND LOCATION

LOCATION OF VISITOR CENTER
Continued

Exit 110

Pros
- Located at the western end of the Badlands National Park Loop Road.
- Possible inclusion into the newly-constructed US Forest Service Visitor Center in Wall, which provides information on the Buffalo Gap National Grassland.
- Existing tourist services.
- Available Federal land.

Cons
- Most visitors would have to back track six miles to Delta Nine, and an additional 11 miles to Delta One.
- NPS experience has shown that a visitor center located away from the resource tends to be underused and less successful.

South Dakota Air and Space Museum, Ellsworth AFB

Pros
- Existing Minuteman missile displays and visitor services.

Cons
- Long distance to missile sites; Delta One is approximately 70 miles east of the museum.
- NPS experience has shown that a visitor center located away from the resource tends to be underused and less successful.

Environmental Assessment

VIEWSHED ANALYSIS

Delta One and Delta Nine are on the American Great Plains, which farmers and ranchers have historically used to graze cattle and cultivate crops. Intermingled with the farm and ranch lands is the Buffalo Gap National Grassland, which is managed by the US Forest Service. As a result, the open landscape surrounding the missile sites is broken only by changes in topography and a few low-profile buildings. Tall vegetation is sparse.

Delta One and Delta Nine blend in with the area's rural character and natural environment. Typical of the local vernacular architecture, Delta One is a one-story, ranch-style complex, painted in a neutral color. Delta Nine is even more unimposing — marked only by a chain link fence, power poles, and radio antennas. When Delta Nine was an active missile silo, the Air Force held a permanent restrictive easement that prohibited houses within a 1,200-foot radius (with some exceptions). Although this easement was acquired for safety reasons, it also created an undisturbed view of the prairie. This easement will terminate when the Air Force sells the property. In order to protect the character of the missile site, this historic viewshed should be preserved.

TOPOGRAPHY

Delta One and Delta Nine are within the northern Great Plains physiographic province, which is characterized by rolling mixed-grass prairie. Elevations range from about 2,550 feet to 2,700 feet.

CLIMATE AND WEATHER

Southwestern South Dakota's climate is semiarid, characterized by hot summers and cold winters. In January, the average minimum temperature is about 7° Fahrenheit; the average high is about 33°. In July, the average maximum temperature is 90°. On average, 13 summer days exceed 100°. Winds of 50 miles per

Left: *Nearly 2,000 persons opposed to nuclear testing staged a demonstration October 28, 1961, near the Soviet Union's United Nations Headquarters Building in New York City, New York.* ASSOCIATED PRESS

hour can occur, most likely in the summer.

Average annual precipitation is 16 inches, falling predominantly in May, June, and July. Thunderstorms are common, and are the main source of spring rainfall. Heavy rains can cause flash flooding along minor tributaries. Yearly snowfall averages 35 inches, and a few heavy snowstorms occur each year. Snow combined with heavy winds can create snowdrifts of several feet, making road maintenance and travel difficult.

SOILS

The soil along Interstate 90 near Delta One and Delta Nine is of the Camborthids-Argiustolls subgroup, which has a clayey texture. The soil shrinks when dry and swells when wet. In dry weather, this type of soil can develop cracks up to two inches wide, 40 inches deep, and several feet long. Load-bearing strength is low. These two qualities of shrink-swell potential and low strength can cause construction limitations. Permeability is very slow to moderate, while runoff is moderate to rapid. Moderate erosion due to either water or wind is a risk. The bedrock type is shale, which may be 30 to 60 inches below the surface.

Near Delta One, south of Exit 127, the soil is in the Weta-Cactusflat association, primarily Weta silt loam, Nunn-Beckton loams, and Cactusflat-Weta complex. These upland soils are generally silty and clayey with a slight alkalinity, and exhibit moderate to severe water and wind erodability. The moderate to high shrink-swell ratings should be considered in the design and construction of buildings. Slow percolation limits the feasibility of septic tank absorption fields while seepage would moderately restrict the use of sewage lagoon areas.

The area northeast of Exit 131 (Cactus Flat) contains soils in the Nunn-Beckton-Hisle association, primarily Larvie-Hisle complex, Metre-Larvie clays, and Orella-Rock outcrop complex, as well as Metre-Hisle complex. The high to very high shrink-swell potential can limit construction. The use of septic tank absorption fields and sewage lagoon areas is severely hindered by the short depth to bedrock. Slow

Several wildlife species, including pronghorn, live in the grasslands near the Delta One and Delta Nine missile sites.

percolation also adversely affects septic tank absorption fields.

VEGETATION

The Interstate 90 corridor from Wall to the turn-off for Badlands National Park at Cactus Flat is within the mixed-grass prairie of the Great Plains. The US Forest Service has conserved the area surrounding the study area as the Buffalo Gap National Grassland. The area is characterized by medium-height grasses, with few areas of shrubs and trees. The dominant grass species are western wheatgrass and green needlegrass. Localized areas can be dominated by short grasses of blue gramma and buffalograss during times of stress. Forbs commonly associated with the mixed grasses include scarlet globemallow, American vetch, prickly pear, and fringed sagewort. Years of higher precipitation can encourage little bluestem bunchgrass.

Shrubs and trees are usually restricted to draws, gullies, and surface waters. Typical shrub species include silver buffaloberry, broom snakeweed, greasewood, and some plum and chokecherry. Cottonwoods, willows, ash, and elms are common tree species growing along streams.

Typical landscape near Delta One.

WILDLIFE

The grasslands along the Interstate 90 study corridor provide habitat for a variety of wildlife species. Large game animals include the pronghorn, mule deer, white-tailed deer, coyote, and bobcat. Among the smaller mammals present are red fox, striped skunk, badger, jackrabbit, prairie dog, and a number of species of other rodents and ground squirrels.

Amphibian and reptile species may include the Great Plains toad, painted turtle, garter snake, and western rattlesnake. US Forest Service sensitive species (that is, species *tending* towards being a candidate for Federal listing as threatened) which are possibly found along Interstate 90 are tiger salamander, northern leopard frog, pale milk snake, northern earless lizard, and northern prairie lizard.

Birds in the area include upland game birds such as pheasant, grouse and turkey. In addition, there are several raptor and hawk species including turkey vultures, eagles, red-tailed hawks, kestrels, ferruginous hawks, Swainson's hawks, prairie falcons, and occasionally peregrine falcons.

Wetland and riparian habitat along the Interstate 90 corridor support shorebirds, waterfowl, and other birds. Species that may be found in some of these habitats include redwing blackbirds, yellow-headed blackbirds, common yellowthroats, snipes, spotted sandpipers, and American avocet. Long-billed curlews (US Forest Service sensitive and previously a candidate for Federal listing) may be present. Species that may be seen near marshes include short-eared owls and another US Forest Service-sensitive species, the northern harrier. Wetlands support a wide variety of migratory waterfowl. Species that may visit these wetlands include coots, Canada geese, herons, whooping cranes, pelicans, and numerous species of ducks.

ENDANGERED, THREATENED, OR CANDIDATE SPECIES

The South Dakota Department of Game, Fish and Parks has not identified any threatened or endangered species within four square miles of Delta One, Delta Nine or Exit 131 (Cactus Flat). All three sites are within or adjacent to the experimental area for black-footed ferret reintroduction. Although the ferret is endangered, it has a reduced status of experimental within this area. Thus, area ranchers can manage prairie dog towns as usual. Since the ferret reintroduction site is about nine miles from Delta Nine, and even farther from Delta One and Exit 131, it is highly unlikely that the missile sites would be considered needed habitat.

FLOOD PLAINS

No flood plain compliance problems are believed to exist at Delta One or Delta Nine.

An intermittent stream course runs south of Exit 127, near Delta One; it drains only about one square mile. At Exit 131 (Cactus Flat), an intermittent stream course runs about 4,000 feet north of the interstate, and drains about two square miles. Both of these areas have flat slopes, good drainage, and small watersheds so only a small amount of water would run through the channels. There should be no problem locating a visitor center outside a flood plain. However, a more thorough examination of these areas should be made before any detailed site planning can occur.

WETLANDS

Both the area south of Interstate 90 at Exit 127 near Delta One, and the public land in the quadrant northeast of Exit 131 (Cactus Flat) have a few small pockets of wetlands. These areas are of the Palustrine emergent system, that is, shallow, nonflowing water in a small area, which supports upright plants. South of Exit 127, County Road 23A curves to avoid an intermittent water course that floods occasionally. Along this water course are two small impounded ponds. Another intermittent water course is located about 4,000 feet north of Exit 131, and a small impounded pond is located on the southern property boundary. It is important to locate any visitor center outside known wetlands.

HAZARDOUS MATERIALS

As part of the deactivation of the 44th Missile Wing, the Air Force will develop a mitigation plan for hazardous materials at the Minuteman facilities, including Delta One and Delta Nine. The National Park Service is working with the Air Force to ensure that the mitigation plan at Delta One and Delta Nine complies with the Secretary of the Interior's Standards for Rehabilitation of Historic Properties and does not destroy the sites' historic character.

Asbestos

Both Delta One and Delta Nine have asbestos-covered plenums that connect diesel electric units with the walls of the containment buildings. Asbestos insulation is also in the exhaust system of the diesel electric units. Delta One may also contain asbestos in the floor tiling and some pipe insulation. At Delta Nine, small quantities of asbestos were found in patching of the sodium chromate tank insulation, electric heater wiring, and electrical switch gear panels.

Polychlorinated Biphenyls (PCBs)

Polychlorinated biphenyls (PCBs) are within electric filters at Delta One and Delta Nine. About 70 of these filters are in the launch tube at Delta Nine. At Delta One, the LCC has lighting and switching filters that may contain PCBs. Three main power filters and approximately 45 load filters are also assumed to contain PCBs.

Sodium Chromate Solution

Sodium chromate solution was used in the coolant system for the missile guidance set. When the system was upgraded in the mid-1980s, two 150-gallon tanks of sodium chromate solution were abandoned in place in the upper level of the launcher equipment room at Delta Nine. The residual in the tanks is less than ten gallons and is likely to be characterized as a hazardous waste.

Diesel Fuel

Diesel was used as a fuel for the back-up generators at Delta Nine and Delta One. If the diesel fuel is used, it is not considered a hazardous waste. However, if the fuel needs to be removed, it would be considered an ignitable hazardous waste.

Lead-based Paint

The Air Force primed and/or painted most interior and exterior surfaces of the Delta Nine launcher and the Delta One LCC with lead-based paint. The paint may contain 20% lead by weight. In addition, other heavy metals such as chromium and mercury may be in the paint. The Air Force removed the lead-based paint from the exterior of Delta Nine.

Pesticides

The Air Force used pesticides, including herbicides and insecticides, at Delta Nine. Herbicides were applied annually since the 1960s. However, the residue levels of herbicides in the soil may be negligible because the chemicals degrade over time. The Air Force also occasionally applied the insecticide Malathion.

Mercury Switches

Thermostats, sump pump controls, water system controls, and air-conditioning controls at Delta One and Delta Nine contain several mercury switches.

Cadmium Electroplating

At Delta One and Delta Nine, the Air Force used cadmium electroplating on several wall mounts, rack supports, and gaskets, each about several square inches.

Underground Storage Tanks

The Delta One LCF has a 1,850-gallon unleaded gasoline underground storage tank, a 12,000-gallon diesel underground storage tank, and a 1,000-gallon heating oil underground storage tank. Delta Nine contains a 2,500-gallon diesel fuel underground storage tank.

Freon (Refrigerant)

Freon, a fluorohydrocarbon, is used in the Delta One and Delta Nine brine chillers, the guidance and control chiller at Delta Nine, and the air conditioning system at the Delta One LCF. An ozone-depleting chemical, freon is a regulated substance.

Diazene

The capillary lines and sensing bulbs of several temperature controllers at the Delta One LF and Delta Nine LCF contain Diazene 42, a brominated benzene product. Although not regulated as a hazardous waste, Diazene 42 is being removed from the other deactivated Minuteman sites.

Batteries

Four lead-acid batteries are used to start the diesel generators at the Delta One LCF and the Delta Nine LF. Two small batteries are used in the power transfer equipment.

Coating Materials

Below-grade surfaces of the support building and launcher at Delta Nine are coated with a poly-vinyl waterproofing spray. The coating contains low levels of PCBs. The diesel USTs and underground piping and conduit at the Delta One LCF and Delta Nine LF are coated with a coal tar/asbestos felt membrane. The felt contains asbestos and the coal tar contains PCBs within the solid matrix.

Petroleum, Oils, and Lubricants (POL)

Various equipment at the Delta One LCF and Delta Nine LF, such as the diesel generators, air compressors, and the hydraulic pumping unit, contain lubricating and hydraulic oils.

Socioeconomic Analysis

REGIONAL OVERVIEW

Delta One is in Jackson County; the county's eastern border is about 46 miles east of the missile site. Delta Nine is in Pennington County; the westernmost segment of Interstate 90 in the county is approximately 64 miles west of the launch facility.

Jackson County, which encompasses more than 1,800 square miles, has a low population for its geographical size. The county seat, Kadoka, is the largest community and had a population of 736 in 1990. Kadoka depends on tourism as well as agriculture, and is a travel stop on the eastern side of Badlands National Park. South of the White River, Jackson County includes a portion of the Pine Ridge Indian Reservation.

Pennington County is the second most populous county in South Dakota. The landscape varies dramatically between the county's eastern and western borders, a distance of just over 100 miles. The western one-third of the county consists of the Black Hills National Forest. Private parcels are interspersed with national forest land, and several vacation travel communities are in the area. Tourism attractions and other facilities are also interspersed in the rural areas of the Black Hills. The eastern two-thirds of Pennington County are largely agricultural, primarily cattle ranching and crop farming. Rapid City, in Pennington County, is the largest city in western South Dakota and had 54,523 people in 1990.

Several small communities are close to Delta Nine in Pennington County. Wall, which has a population of 834, is the nearest community. Wall's economy is dominated by tourism, and benefits from being near the western entrance to Badlands National Park. The town is also home to well-known Wall Drug. Wasta and New Underwood are located between Wall and Rapid City and had populations of 82 and 553, respectively, in 1990.

Table 1 summarizes socioeconomic characteristics of Jackson and Pennington Counties. As it shows, the two counties are dramatically different. Pennington County is dominated by Rapid City and its immediate area of influence. Out of a total county population of 81,361, approximately 65,000 to 70,000 people reside in the Rapid City area. In the 1980s, Pennington County grew by almost 16%, while Jackson County's population fell by 16%. Per capita income is almost twice as high in urban-

---

Left: *Construction of a Minuteman launch facility.* US ARMY CORPS OF ENGINEERS

TABLE 1
SOCIOECONOMIC CHARACTERISTICS OF JACKSON AND PENNINGTON COUNTIES

	Jackson	Pennington
1980 Population	3,347	70,361
1990 Population	2,811	81,343
% Change Population 1980-90	-16.0%	+15.6%
Per Capita Income 1989	$6,947	$12,031
Household Income 1989	$21,188	$31,697
% Below Poverty Level (Pop.)	12.9%	8.8%
Number Employed 1990	1,001	36,145
Unemployment Rate 1990	10.6%	5.8%

SOURCE: US Bureau of the Census, 1980 and 1990.

TABLE 2
SOCIOECONOMIC CHARACTERISTICS OF KADOKA AND WALL, SOUTH DAKOTA

	Kadoka	Wall
1980 Population	832	770
1990 Population	736	834
% Change Population 1980-90	-11.5%	+8.3%
Per Capita Income 1989	$9,759	$12,851
Household Income 1989	$23,074	$31,039
Taxable Sales 1992	$8.5 Million	$21.7 Million*
Number Employed 1990	387	406
Unemployment Rate 1990	5.2%	0.7%

SOURCE: US Bureau of the Census, 1980 and 1990.
* Taxable sales in Wall excludes utilities.

TABLE 3
EMPLOYMENT BY INDUSTRY, JACKSON AND PENNINGTON COUNTIES

	Jackson		Pennington	
	Number	Percent	Number	Percent
Agric. Fish & For.	280	28.0%	912	2.5%
Mining	0	0.0%	269	0.7%
Construction	80	8.0%	2,543	7.0%
Manufacturing	16	1.6%	4,174	11.5%
Transportation	28	2.8%	1,360	3.8%
Comm. & Pub. Utilities	11	1.1%	863	2.4%
Wholesale Trade	29	2.9%	1,433	4.0%
Retail Trade	173	17.3%	7,653	21.1%
Fin., Ins. & Real Estate	34	3.4%	1,797	5.0%
Educational Services	149	14.9%	3,287	9.1%
Other Services	109	10.9%	9,768	27.0%
Public Administration	92	9.2%	2,177	6.0%
Totals	1,001		36,236	

SOURCE: US Bureau of the Census, 1980 and 1990.

dominated Pennington County as it is in rural Jackson County. Household income is more than $10,000 higher in Pennington compared to Jackson County. In 1990, the unemployment rate in Pennington County was about half of that in Jackson County.

A more representative picture of the socioeconomic characteristics surrounding Delta One and Delta Nine may be seen in Table 2, which focuses on Wall and Kadoka, the two closest communities. Wall is 17 miles west of Delta One, and six miles west of Delta Nine. Kadoka is 23 miles east of Delta One.

Populations moved in opposite directions in these two communities in the 1980s. Per capita and household incomes in Kadoka are higher than in the balance of Jackson County, but considerably lower than corresponding measures in Wall. Income measures in Wall are nearly the same as is found in the balance of Pennington County. Unemployment was virtually nonexistent in Wall in 1990.

Taxable sales in Wall are adjusted to exclude regional sales by the West River Electric Cooperative. Even so, taxable sales in Wall are two to three times higher than those in Kadoka. However, both towns experienced significant growth in taxable sales over the last four years, exceeding 7% annually. Most of this growth can be directly traced to the vacation travel industry.

Table 3 shows the distribution of jobs by industry for Jackson and Pennington Counties. Jackson County has a much higher proportion of its work force in agriculture, but a smaller percentage in manufacturing. Pennington County's diversified economy yields relatively more jobs in the service sectors.

THE VACATION TRAVEL INDUSTRY

Interstate 90, which passes through all of Jackson and most of Pennington Counties, is the major carrier of tourists into the Black Hills. This area of South Dakota has a diversified tourism industry that relies on its scenic and historic resources, as well as gaming in Deadwood. In addition, Interstate 90 carries visitors to Yellowstone and Glacier National Parks, as well as other destinations west of the South Dakota border. Mount Rushmore Na-

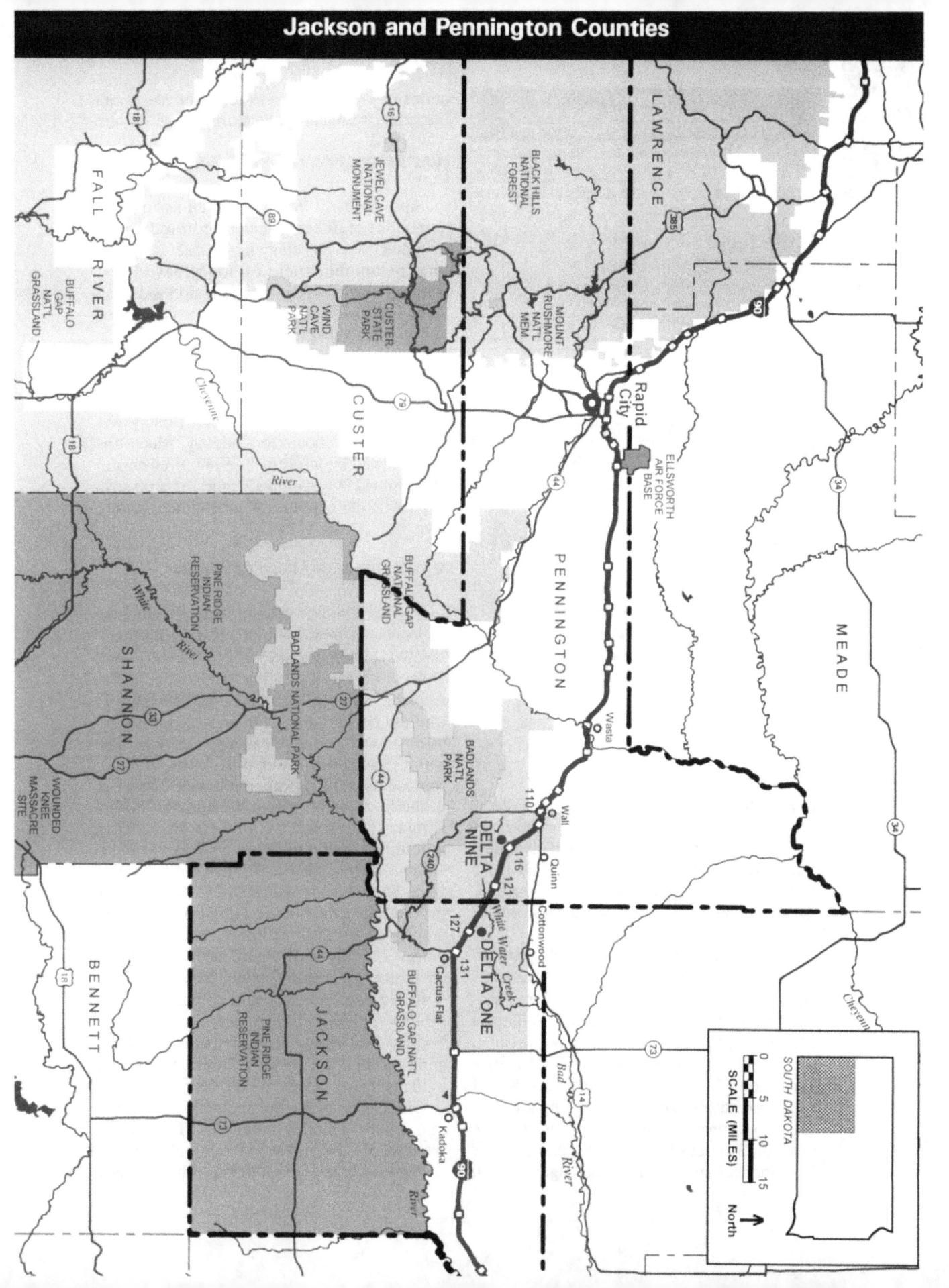

MINUTEMAN SPECIAL RESOURCE STUDY

TABLE 4
ANNUAL VISITATIONS, SELECTED WESTERN SOUTH DAKOTA LOCATIONS

Year	Mt. Rushmore Nat'l Mem.	Wind Cave Nat'l Park	Custer State Park	Badlands Nat'l Park
1988	2,013,749	1,187,631	1,010,880	1,117,931*
1989	2,075,190	1,127,025	1,032,403	1,249,956*
1990	2,161,965	1,169,656	1,245,465	1,326,435*
1991	2,681,928	1,181,233	1,425,945	1,196,623
1992	2,586,785	1,304,007	1,494,400	1,433,230
1993	2,601,415	749,303	1,492,383	1,356,558
Ave. Growth	5.3%	2.4%**	8.1%	3.9%

SOURCE: Statistical Records of Each Facility.
* Fiscal Year Data.
** 1988-1992 Growth Rate, 1993 Visitation affected by heavy road construction.

TABLE 5
ANNUAL VISITOR EXPENDITURES, JACKSON AND PENNINGTON COUNTIES, 1985-1992

Year	Jackson	Pennington
1985	$2,809,111	$64,452,463
1986	$4,602,517	$65,514,803
1987	$4,711,329	$69,074,830
1988	$4,773,747	$74,523,148
1989	$5,307,735	$88,996,912
1990	$6,780,550	$98,894,765
1991	$7,193,164	$112,471,412
1992	$8,009,349	$108,723,892
Average % Change	+ 15.8%	+ 9.8%

SOURCE: Economic and Fiscal Impacts Associated with the Vacation Travel Industry in South Dakota, Michael K. Madden, 1992.

tional Memorial, Wind Cave National Park, and Custer State Park are three of the most popular points of interest. Badlands National Park, which is south of Delta One and Delta Nine, is also a very popular natural attraction. Table 4 shows recent visitation at these attractions.

Intra-year visitation rates at these destinations are seasonal, as is travel activity in western South Dakota. June through September visitations account for 81% of the annual volume at Mount Rushmore and 63% at Wind Cave. Corresponding percentages for Custer State Park and Badlands National Park are 70% and 83% respectively. The climate largely accounts for the seasonal nature of the travel industry. Over the last decade, September and October have increasingly become more significant in terms of visitor volume as retirees make up an increasing segment of the tourism base.

VACATION TRAVEL SPENDING

Since the early 1980s, the South Dakota Department of Tourism has monitored travel spending for each county in the state — including the amount spent on food, beverages, lodging, entertainment, transportation and retail goods. Table 5 shows the visitor expenditures for Jackson and Pennington Counties.

When inflationary impacts are removed, average annual real growth in Jackson County has been 11.9% since 1985. During the same period, real growth in Pennington County was 5.9%. The vacation travel industry, which was strengthened by infrastructure improvements in Jackson and Pennington Counties, is a positive aspect of the economic environment of the area.

VEHICULAR TRAFFIC PATTERNS

The correlation between visitor volume at regional attractions and traffic patterns on Interstate 90 is illustrated in Graph 1. Exit 116, near Delta Nine, has a full-time, automatic, traffic recorder. Since there are no exits with significant use between Exits 116 and 127, it can be assumed that the traffic passing each exit is the same. The solid, lower portion of Graph 1 represents traffic volume that would exist if traffic in all months were the same as that in January, the lowest volume month. This amount of traffic is referenced as the base volume and is equal to 713,000 vehicles per year. The vertical bars represent the seasonal movements above the low month base. The amplitude of traffic volume is clearly illustrated. The July and August monthly traffic is about three times the monthly base of 59,427. It should be noted that local, commercial, and other vehicular traffic also rises above the January base during the year, but it is equally apparent that the bulk of the annual rise in traffic is traced to vacation travelers.

Graph 2 converts the above traffic counts into relative monthly influences. The annual seasonal rise is calculated as the residual above the January base for each month. The residuals

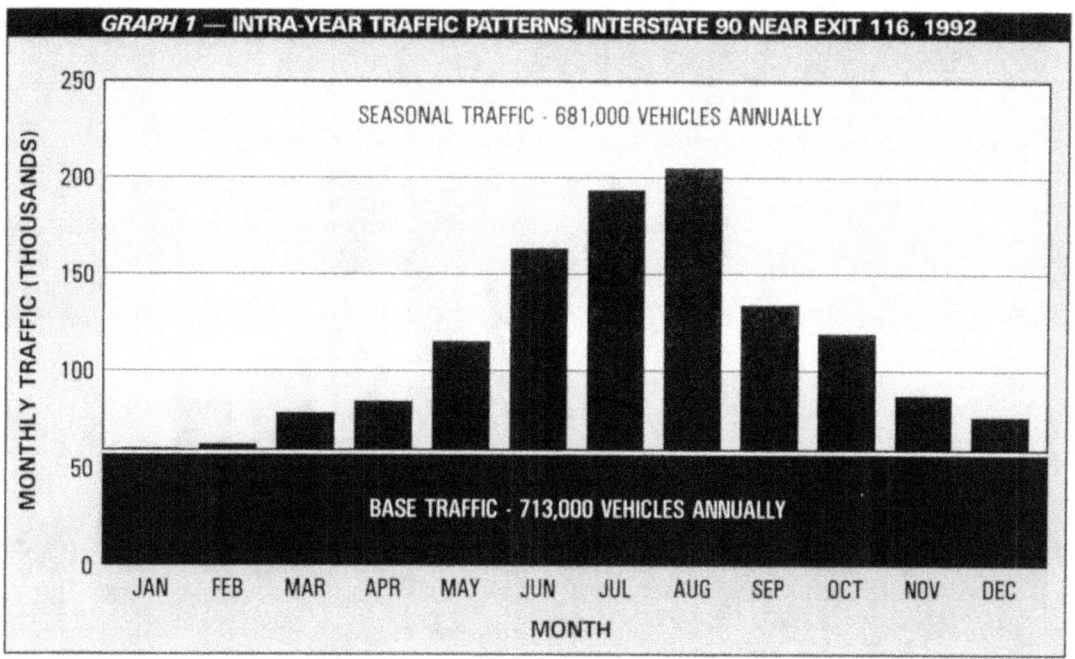

GRAPH 1 — INTRA-YEAR TRAFFIC PATTERNS, INTERSTATE 90 NEAR EXIT 116, 1992

then are converted into percentages. July and August have the highest relative seasonal volume, followed by June, September, and October in descending order.

It must be noted that the traffic counter is at Exit 116, which is between the exits that lead to Highway 240, the Badlands National Park Loop Road. As a result, a great deal of traffic bypasses the traffic counter. Badlands National Park estimates that an additional 400,000 vehicles take the Badlands National Park Loop Road. Thus, approximately 37% of Interstate 90's seasonal traffic is diverted through the national park, and does not pass either Delta One or Delta Nine, which are located at Exits 127 and 116 respectively.

VISITATION POTENTIAL AT MINUTEMAN MISSILE NATIONAL HISTORIC SITE

Visitation potential at the proposed Minuteman Missile National Historic Site is related to the available traffic volume passing the visitor center — but only in the sense that the existing traffic guarantees that prospective visitors are available. From a marketing and promotion perspective, this has important implications because it shows that visitors do not need to be attracted to the area, but rather diverted from Interstate 90.

Visitation would also be affected by the type and location of the visitor center. For the purposes of this study, Exit 131 was selected to provide a baseline estimate for projected visitation. A preliminary analysis indicates that a Minuteman Missile National Historic Site Visitor Center at Exit 131 near Cactus Flat (which is four miles east of Delta One and 15 miles east of Delta Nine) would attract the greatest number of visitors. Exit 131 is the major entrance and exit point for Badlands National Park, which is visited by approximately 1.2 to 1.4 million people each year. In addition, travelers use Exit 131 to drive south to the Pine Ridge Indian Reservation. As the proposed development of the Wounded Knee historic site progresses toward completion, more and more travelers can be expected to be diverted to the reservation.

Approximately 400,000 vehicles travel the Badlands National Park Loop Road each year, and another 680,000 vehicles bypass the national park on Interstate 90. A significant, but undetermined, number of these vehicles carry travelers who are on return trips from their primary destination. Because it is unlikely that tourists would visit the Minuteman Missile

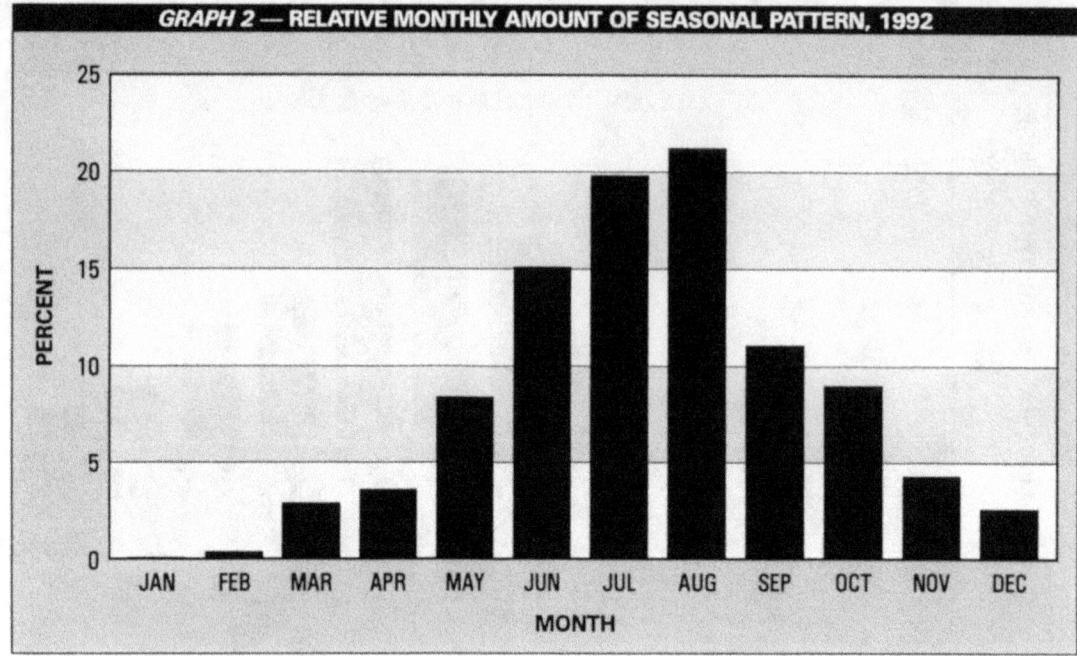

Visitor Center both as they enter and exit the region, the total number of 1,080,000 vehicles must be adjusted downward. In order that the visitation potential is not overstated, it is assumed that the effective number of available vehicles is 750,000, representing about 2.1 million people. This adjustment is usually not necessary in this type of analysis but, in the case of South Dakota, the travel market is heavily concentrated in states to the east, most of which use Interstate 90 for both their departure and return trips.

Projections of visitation are based on reasonable capture rates of available visitors in proximity to the facility. In this case, the effective number of travelers is assumed to be 2.1 million. This number can be compared to the capture rates at other National Park Service units. In 1993, visitation to the south unit of Theodore Roosevelt National Park was about 401,000. Attendance at the visitor center was 170,000. Traffic counts on Interstate 94, the major highway to Theodore Roosevelt National Park, were estimated at 1,379,470. The capture rate to the park itself was 29.1%, and 12.3% at the visitor center.

A similar analysis was made at the Little Bighorn Battlefield National Monument in southeast Montana. Although Little Bighorn's visitor center is not as extensive as those at Theodore Roosevelt or Badlands National Parks, approximately 335,330 people visited the monument in 1993. Approximately 1.3 million vacationers traveled Interstate 90 and Highway 212 near Little Bighorn — which implies a capture rate of 25.8%.

At Badlands National Park, a yearly visitation of 1.25 million out of the 2.1 million potential visitors available on Interstate 90 implies a capture rate of about 60%. Park officials documented 294,000 people at the visitor center in 1993. This represents about 24% of all park visitation, and 14% of all available tourist traffic on Interstate 90.

EXIT 131 VISITOR CENTER ESTIMATES

As outlined above, the experiences of other National Park Service units suggest that the capture rate of the proposed Minuteman Missile National Historic Site Visitor Center at Exit 131 is likely to be in the range of 11-15%. This range is also consistent with National Park Service facilities in the Black Hills region. Based on an available population of 2.1 million tourists, the visitation to the Minuteman Missile National Historic Site is estimated in Table 6. The five and ten-years estimates of future visi-

TABLE 6 PROJECTED VISITATION, EXIT 131 VISITOR CENTER		
Year	Low Range	High Range
Initial Year	231,000	315,000
5 Years Later	307,000	418,000
10 Years Later	409,000	556,000

tation are based on the historical growth rate of the travel industry in western South Dakota.

Based on a midpoint projection, approximately 362,500 people would visit a multi-resource visitor center at Exit 131 five years after opening. However, it is important to note that only about 45% of this number represents *new* visitors — an incremental increase above the normal visitation at Badlands National Park. On average, these visitors would spend an extra half day in the area. Thus, it is estimated that a multi-resource visitor center at Exit 131 would receive approximately 163,000 *new* half-day visitations per year.

Actual attendance, of course, will be affected by a wide variety of factors. The management structure, pricing, advertising strategies, and ability to cross-market among other attractions will be critical determinants in ultimate attendance. Outside displays and travel amenities are also important visitation factors.

Summary of Public Responses

This is a rare opportunity for the National Park Service to interpret the Cold War and nuclear arms race, a story that currently is not being told within the NPS system . . . Inclusion of the Minuteman II site would ensure that an important era of human history in America is preserved and interpreted for future generations.

— Lori M. Nelson, Regional Director
National Parks and Conservation Association

South Dakotans have been very supportive of the presence of Ellsworth Air Force Base and the Minuteman Missile . . . We would continue to work hard in supporting the efforts of the National Park Service in preserving and interpreting the history of the Minuteman Missile system.

— Jim Quinn, Executive Director
Historic South Dakota Foundation

The National Park Service has a proven track record of preserving and managing historic sites of national significance. They have the commitment and resources needed to make this project a successful tribute to the role ICBMs and missileers played during the Cold War.

— Arlen D. Jameson, Lieutenant General, USAF
Deputy Commander in Chief US Strategic Command

Left: *In an effort to involve local residents in the planning process for Delta One and Delta Nine, the National Park Service held two public meetings in South Dakota. In Wall on January 25, 1994, local residents shared their views with the study team.* RICHARD M. KOHEN

The Wall City Council members unanimously support the preservation of the Minuteman Missile history.

— David L. Hahn, Mayor

This preservation is highly significant. We must preserve this story in hopes of preventing this sort of hell from happening again. Time will make this project far more important than it seems now.

— Paul Jensen, Wall

Development and deployment of Minuteman was a great example of the value of long-range development — both for national defense and economic prosperity. Such development is sadly lacking today . . .

— Edward N. Hall
Colonel USAF, Ret., and Director of the Minuteman Missile Program, 1954-1958

I feel this is the best way to preserve a part of our history for us and generations to come.

— Tammy S. Niemann, Philip, South Dakota

Although a Colorado resident now, far removed from the western South Dakota Minuteman sites, I grew up on the edge of the Badlands in Jackson County . . . I support Alternative 3 as I believe these sites are truly of national historic interest and I also firmly believe that the National Park Service is the logical choice of an entity to preserve and interpret them.

— Merle E. Crew, Grand Junction, Colorado

It would be a terrible loss to the youth of our country to allow this information to disappear from our history.

— Donald G. Regas, Philip

Tourism is South Dakota's second most important industry, and we are striving to attract more people to our state with an expanding emphasis on the many things we have to offer. I can see nothing but benefit, for both South Dakotans and visitors, by giving them the opportunity to see a missile site as it existed in a state of preparedness. In that vein, I believe it is important that the site not only be preserved, but also be designated as a National Historic Site.

— Roger Porch, Senator, South Dakota

The Association of Air Force Missileers strongly supports the National Park Service project to establish the Cold War memorial using Minuteman missile facilities Delta One and Delta Nine . . .

— Charles G. Simpson, Colonel, USAF (Retired)

I am convinced that these sites are highly deserving of preservation and interpretation by the National Park Service, and would provide an unmatched opportunity to educate the public on Cold War historical themes.

— Mark Hufstetler, Butte, Montana

PUBLIC PARTICIPATION PROCESS

The public played an important role in evaluating the possible preservation of Delta One and Delta Nine, and developing the management alternatives that are presented here. In December 1993, in an effort to encourage public participation, the National Park Service sent an informational brochure to over 400 citizens and organizations. Press releases, radio and television interviews, and articles in national and local publications also disseminated information about the project. In early 1994, the National Park Service held two public open houses in South Dakota — in Wall on January 25, and in Rapid City on January 26 — at which local residents shared their views with study team members.

In July 1994, the National Park Service mailed a *Preliminary Management Alternatives* brochure to over 600 people. The brochure briefly described the three preliminary alternatives: Alternative 1 (No-Action), Alternative 2 (A non-NPS organization preserves Delta One and Delta Nine), and Alternative 3 (Delta One and Delta Nine become a National Historic Site). The brochure included a self-mailing response form, on which people were asked to select their preferred alternative. The questionnaire also asked for comments on how the alternatives could be improved, as well as the best location for a potential Minuteman Missile National Historic Site Visitor Center.

Eighty-nine people filled out and returned the questionnaire. Overall, the Minuteman Special Resource Study Team heard from people across the Nation. Although most of the people were from South Dakota, responses were also received from Alabama, California, Colorado, Florida, Maryland, Minnesota, Montana, Nebraska, New Mexico, North Carolina, Pennsylvania, Tennessee, Virginia, Wisconsin, and Washington D.C.

Of the 89 people who filled out the questionnaire, approximately 91% supported the preservation of Delta One and Delta Nine. Approximately 86.5% endorsed the National Park Service acquisition of Delta One and Delta Nine as a National Historic Site (Alternative 3), while 4.5% wanted an organization other than the National Park Service to manage the missile sites (Alternative 2). Approximately 9% supported "no action" (Alternative 1).

PUBLIC SUPPORT FOR THE MANAGEMENT ALTERNATIVES

Alternative 3 —
Public Support: 86.5%

Alternative 3 received the greatest support. Of the 89 responses, 77 supported National Park Service acquisition of Delta One and Delta Nine as a National Historic Site. Overwhelmingly, supporters of Alternative 3 were convinced of the need to preserve the Minuteman sites, and believed the National Park Service could provide the best measure of protection and interpretation. Typical responses:

The National Park Service has personnel at its disposal who are experienced in managing national historic sites . . .

non-profit and other non-governmental entities may not have the expertise or internal policies and guidelines to assist them with prudent management of the resource.

The National Park Service has a proven management track record and, hopefully, the financial resources to do the job right.

Site management by the NPS ensures stability, continuity, and a constant presence at the site, not to mention a certain degree of federal funding . . .

A non-profit probably could not handle it because of complication in "red tape" with the Air Force Museum and with finding volunteers to work in that location.

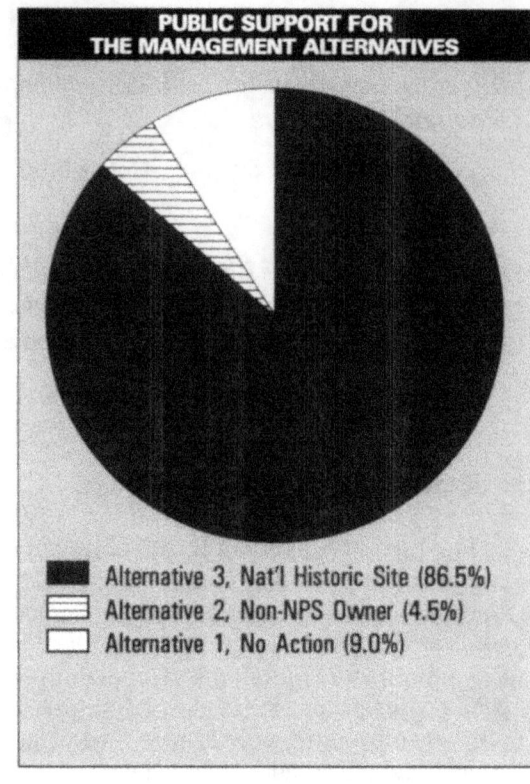

Others saw National Park Service management of Delta One and Delta Nine as the best way to facilitate cooperation among Badlands National Park, the US Forest Service, a possible Wounded Knee National Tribal Park, and other governmental entities.

Alternative 2 —
Public Support: 4.5%

Four people supported Alternative 2, which called for a non-National Park Service entity to take over the preservation of Delta One and Delta Nine. One respondent suggested that the Air Force preserve Delta One and Delta Nine and operate it as a museum (although the Air Force has declined this option). There were no other suggestions for new owners. In general, supporters of Alternative 2 were concerned about Federal spending and efficiency.

Alternative 1 —
Public Support: 9%

Eight people supported Alternative 1, the "no action" plan that would result in the destruction of Delta One and Delta Nine. The reasons were mixed. Some people objected to the preservation of Delta One and Delta Nine for pacifist reasons. "Let's not glorify weaponry," wrote one local resident, suggesting instead that we "pound swords into plowshares."

Another person asked: "Who wants to be reminded of the Cold War — especially on the prairies of South Dakota?"

Others saw the preservation of the missile sites as an unnecessary Federal expense, and wanted the land to revert to agricultural use. "I don't want to be reminded of what they stood for," wrote one person about Delta One and Delta Nine, "let's remove the past and go the future." Two people felt that the exhibits at the South Dakota Air and Space Museum provided enough interpretation of the Minuteman experience.

MINUTEMAN MISSILE NATIONAL HISTORIC SITE VISITOR CENTER:
A Stand-Alone or Multi-Resource Center?

Thirty-six questionnaire respondents had opinions as to whether the proposed Minuteman Missile National Historic Site Visitor Center should be a stand-alone facility that focuses on the Minuteman ICBM, the Cold War, and the arms race — or a multi-resource center that also includes information on other

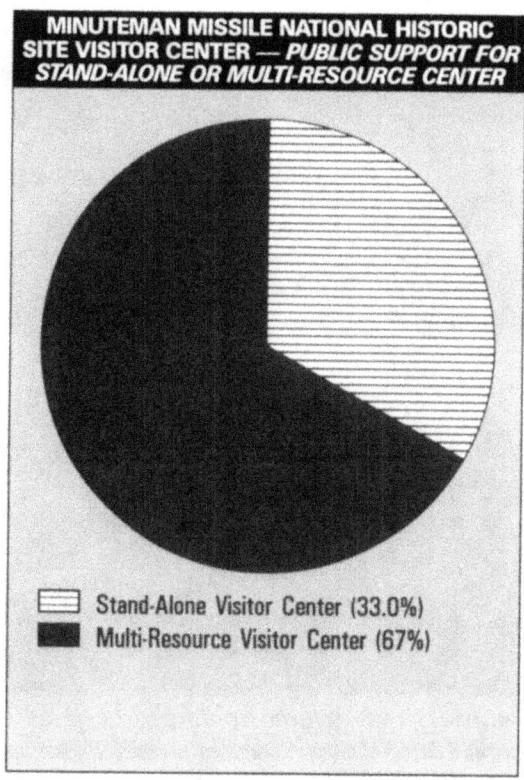
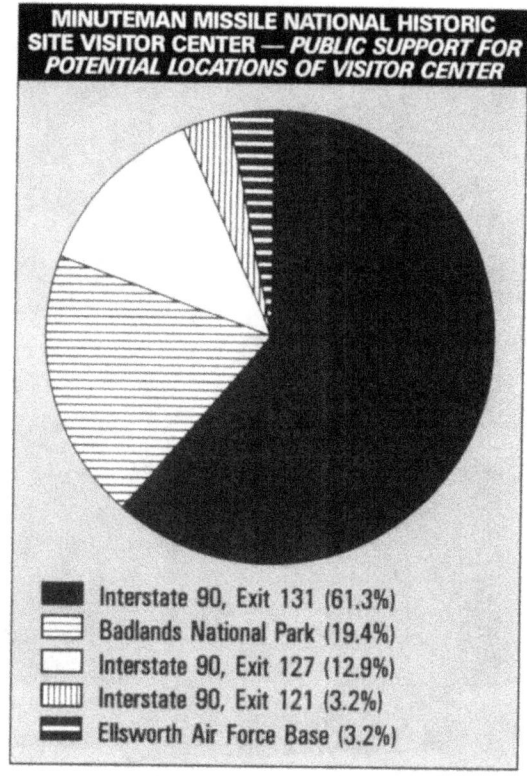

aspects of the Great Plains.

Twelve people preferred a stand-alone visitor center. Most of these respondents felt that a stand-alone center would offer a better interpretive experience. "Because it would focus solely on the Minuteman sites, [the stand-alone center] would offer an exclusive, undiluted interpretation," wrote one person. Another supporter commented that it would be "difficult to provide a unified approach to the history of the Great Plains in one visitor center." "Big Foot's Trail and the entire Wounded Knee massacre site deserve an interpretive exhibit all unto itself," said one person. Another person believed that a "single facility [for Minuteman] also makes the most economic sense."

Twenty-four of the 36 people who had an opinion as to the best type of visitor center supported the concept of a multi-resource facility. Most saw it as a way to save money, particularly in terms of construction and overhead costs. One person questioned if the government should build a Minuteman Missile Visitor Center in an area that already has several Federally-operated centers — including those at Badlands National Park, Mount Rushmore National Memorial, and the US Forest Service Visitor Center in Wall.

Several respondents also offered opinions on how to interpret the Minuteman missile experience. Among the responses:

As part of the story, the viewpoint of the local ranchers and farmers needs to be told.

Stress the history and significance of Minuteman relative to U.S. engineering industry and prosperity of the nation . . .

The actual physical remnants from the Russian equivalent of Minuteman would add a great deal to the interpretive center.

Consult with the Holocaust Museum on how to portray the negative sides of human history . . . The arms race is something to learn from — to study our mistakes not to glorify our stupidity.

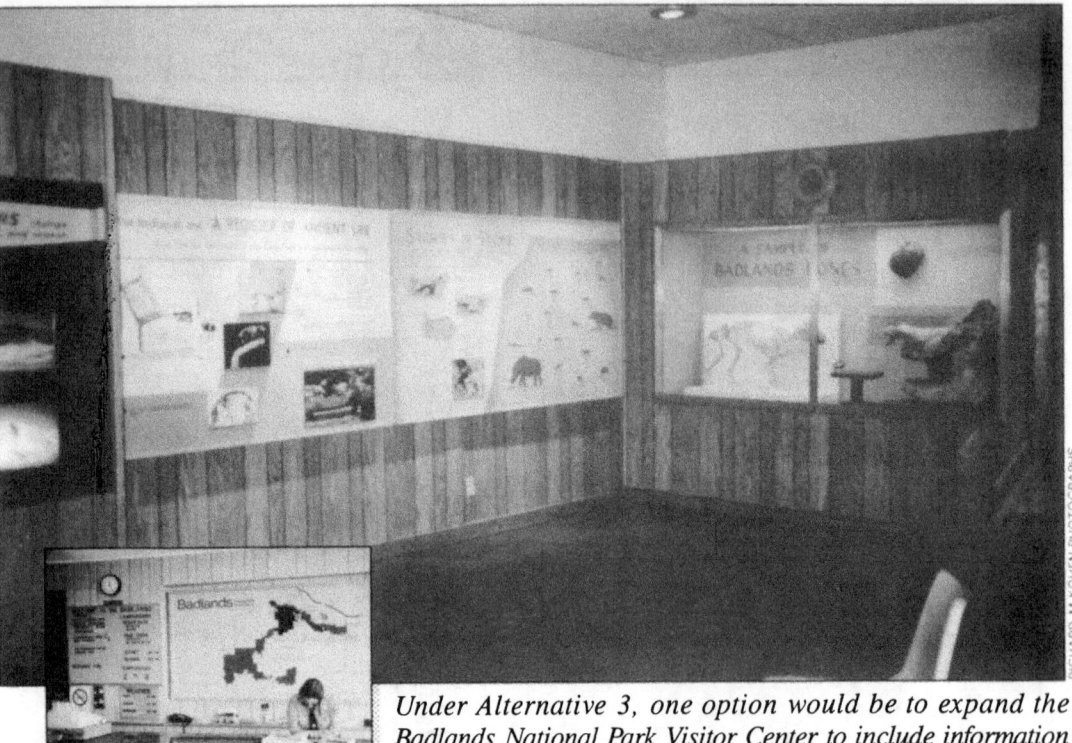

Under Alternative 3, one option would be to expand the Badlands National Park Visitor Center to include information on the Minuteman Missile National Historic Site.

The daily routine of missileers should be told at the visitor center or during a shuttle bus ride to Delta One. This should include arrival times at the support base, pre-task and pre-departure briefings . . . If possible, obtain Air Force vehicles to place on the sites to enhance realism.

Preferred Location of the Visitor Center

Thirty-one respondents also offered recommendations on the best location for a potential Minuteman Missile Visitor Center. Of these, 19 (61.3%) chose Exit 131, six (19.4%) chose Badlands National Park, and four (12.9%) chose Exit 127. Exits 121 and Ellsworth Air Force Base each received one endorsement.

Exit 131. A visitor center at Exit 131 received the greatest support. Most respondents chose this exit because it was at the beginning of the Badlands National Park Loop Road. One supporter echoed a popular sentiment when he wrote that "Exit 131 is in close proximity to Delta One without visually intruding on it, and would reach visitors who otherwise miss the Minuteman site by choosing to travel west on the Loop road . . ." Another person stated: "Exit 131 would be the most appropriate choice . . . Badlands Loop 240 begins there, and this exit bears the most traffic." Several people noted the proximity of existing tourist facilities to Exit 131. The majority of Exit 131 supporters also believed that the visitor center should be a multi-resource facility. Typical responses:

A new visitor center placed here would be a real asset to the tourist, as its strategic location could provide a plethora of information not only about the Badlands, but about the other sites the tourist would be interested in as well, such as the missile sites and Big Foot Trail.

The high traffic to the Badlands National Park furnishes the greatest exposure for the visitor center and Exit 131 already has commercial facilities that would additionally help build the patronage necessary for the visitor center and sites to become a success.

Exit 121 and Exit 127 would both miss a major portion of the tourist traffic that would have already turned off on the Badlands Loop.

Several people were also concerned that local businesses would suffer if a new visitor center were constructed anywhere other than Exit 131. "The local economy would be devastated if a visitor center was located at Exit 121 or 127," said one respondent. "In the rural area that we live in, it is of great importance to keep the established businesses going, as a large portion of the money made at businesses along the Badlands Loop is spent in the communities of Wall, Kadoka, and Philip."

Badlands National Park. The next most popular location for the Minuteman Missile National Historic Site Visitor Center was at Badlands National Park, which was endorsed by six respondents. Some people saw this as an opportunity to upgrade and/or replace the existing visitor center. "A new visitor center should be built for Badlands National Park, and could easily be made to incorporate the missile sites," wrote one person.

Exit 127. Four people endorsed a visitor center at Exit 127, generally because it is the closest exit to Delta One. Two respondents felt it should be a stand-alone center; the other two believed it should be a multi-resource facility.

One person suggested that the best location for a Minuteman Missile Visitor Center would be at Ellsworth Air Force Base, perhaps in conjunction with the South Dakota Air and Space Museum. Another person suggested Exit 121, and advised to "not get the site too close to the Badlands Route to Park . . . This would become too crowded and it would get lost in 'things to do.' "

Bibliography

BOOKS

Brands, H.W., Jr. *Cold Warriors*. New York: Columbia University Press, 1988.

Diggins, John Patrick. *The Proud Decades: America in War and Peace, 1941-1960*. New York: W.W. Norton, 1989.

Jensen, Kenneth M. *Origins of the Cold War: The Novikov, Kennan, and Roberts "Long Telegrams" of 1946*. Washington, D.C.: United States Institute of Peace, 1991.

Kaplan, Fred. *Wizards of Armageddon*. Stanford, CA: Stanford University Press, 1991.

Neal, Roy. *Ace in the Hole*. Garden City, NY: Doubleday & Company, Inc., 1962.

Neufeld, Jacob. *The Development of Ballistic Missiles in the United States Air Force, 1945-1960*. Washington, D.C.: Office of Air Force History, 1990.

Perry, Robert L. "The Atlas, Thor, Titan, and Minuteman." In *The History of Rocket Technology*, edited by Eugene M. Emme. Detroit: Wayne State University Press, 1964.

Prados, John. *The Soviet Estimate*. New York: Dial Press, 1982.

Pursell, Carroll W., Jr., ed. *Readings in Technology and American Life*. New York: Oxford University Press, 1969.

SAC Missile Chronology, 1939-1982. Offutt AFB, NE: Office of the Historian, HQ Strategic Air Command, 1983.

Schwiebert, Ernest G. *A History of the U.S. Air Force Ballistic Missiles*. New York: Frederick A. Praeger, 1965.

PERIODICALS

"Closing The Gap." *Time* 77 (10 February 1961): 16-17.

"End of the Cold War." *The CQ Researcher* 2 (21 August 1992): 721.

Left: *Minuteman missile, first stage thrusters.* ROBERT LYON

Griswold, Wesley S. "Minuteman, Our Ace in the Hole." *Popular Science* 179 (July 1961): 62-65, 184.

"Home of the Minuteman." *Time* 75 (25 January 1960): 48-49.

Kennan, George. "The Sources of Soviet Conduct." *Foreign Affairs* 25 (July 1947): 566-582.

Licklider, Roy. "The Missile Gap Controversy." *Political Science Quarterly* 85 (December 1979): 600-15.

Miller, Barry. "ICBMs Get Major Modification." *Aviation Week and Space Technology* 104 (10 May 1976): 67-70.

"Minuteman II Emplacement Cost to Top $1 Billion." *Missiles and Rockets* 16 (24 May, 1965): 12.

Plattner, C.M. "First SAC Crews Controlling Minuteman." *Aviation Week and Space Technology* 78 (7 January 1963): 62-63, 65.

"Soviet Satellite Sends U.S. in Tizzy." *Life* 43 (October 14, 1957): 34-37

Stolley, Richard B. "How It Feels to Hold the Nuclear Trigger." *Life* 57 (6 November 1957): 34-41.

Stone, Irving. "Companies Vie for Minuteman Contract." *Aviation Week* 68 (17 March 1958): 18-19.

Taylor, Hal. "McNamara Voices Some Optimism over Nike-X, Tells Minuteman Plans." *Missiles and Rockets* 14 (3 February 1964): 20-21.

NEWSPAPERS AND MAGAZINES

New York Times, various years.

Rapid City Daily Journal, various years.

Wall Street Journal, various years.

UNPUBLISHED

Binder, Michael S. Historic American Engineering Record (draft), Minuteman II ICBM, Ellsworth AFB, Launch Control Facility D-1, and Launch Facility D-9. 1993. On file at the National Park Service, Rocky Mountain Region.

Lauber, John F. Minuteman ICBM National Historic Landmark nomination form. 1994. On file at the National Park Service, Rocky Mountain Region.

Lauber, John F. and Jeffrey A. Hess. Historic American Engineering Record, Glenn L. Martin Company, Titan Missile Test Facilities. 1993. HAER Number CO-75.

Reed, George A. "U.S. Defense Policy, U.S. Air Force Doctrine and Strategic Nuclear Weapon Systems, 1958-1964: The Case of the Minuteman ICBM." Ph.D. dissertation. Durham, NC: Duke University, 1986.

INTERVIEWS

Bowen, Mark (Lieutenant). Minuteman launch crew training specialist. Interviewed by John F. Lauber, 5 November 1993, Ellsworth AFB.

Hockaday, David (Lt. Col.). Commander, 44th Operations Support Squadron, Ellsworth AFB. Phone interview by John Lauber, 17 December 1993.

Pavek, Tim. Missile engineer with the 28 Civil Engineering Squadron, Ellsworth AFB. Interviewed by John F. Lauber on 5 and 12 November 1993, Ellsworth AFB. Telephone interview by John Lauber, 28 February 1994.

Schriever, Bernard A. (General). Former commander of Western Development Division. Interviewed by Maj. Lyn R. Officer and Dr. James C. Hasdorff, 20 June 1973, Washington, D.C. Transcript in collection of USAF Historical Research Agency, Maxwell AFB, AL. File K239.0512-783.

ARCHIVAL SOURCES

Air Force Historical Research Agency, Maxwell AFB, AL. Miscellaneous records pertaining to the American ICBM program.

Ballistic Missile Organization History Office, Norton AFB, San Bernardino, CA. Miscellaneous records pertaining to the ICBM program in general and to the Minuteman program in particular.

28 Civil Engineering Squadron, Ellsworth AFB. Architectural and engineering drawings, blueprints and site plans of Minuteman facilities at Ellsworth. Original real estate records, construction completion reports, and other miscellaneous documents relating to the Minuteman deployment at Ellsworth AFB.

44th Missile Wing History Office, Ellsworth AFB. Unit histories and other records relating to the Minuteman activities at Ellsworth AFB.

ENVIRONMENTAL ASSESSMENT — PERSONS AND AGENCIES CONTACTED

Backlund, Douglas. Natural Heritage Program, South Dakota Department of Game, Fish and Parks.

Bessken, Bruce P. Chief of Resource Management, Badlands National Park, National Park Service.

McDonald, Peter. Buffalo Gap National Grassland, US Forest Service.

Office of Climate and Weather Information, South Dakota State University.

Rungee, Russell. Badlands National Park, National Park Service.

Smiley, Gary. Water Resources Division, National Park Service.

Zschomler, Stan. South Dakota Field Office, US Fish and Wildlife Service.

Minuteman Special Resource Study Team Members

NATIONAL PARK SERVICE

Gregory Kendrick, Team Leader

Ben Hawkins, Electrical Engineer
A. Sayre Hutchison, Architect
Richard M. Kohen, Visual Information Specialist
Robert Lyon, Photographer
Irv Mortenson, Superintendent, Badlands National Park
Connie Rudd, Interpretive Planner
Ramona Ruhl, Graphics & Research Assistant
Cathy Sacco, Landscape Architect
Lysa Wegman-French, Natural Resource Analyst
Christine Whitacre, Editor
Joseph W. Zarki, Chief of Interpretation, Badlands National Park

CONSULTANTS

Ron Alley, Director, South Dakota Air and Space Museum
John F. Lauber, Hess, Roise and Company
Michael K. Madden, Economist
Lori M. Nelson, Regional Director, Heartland Regional Office
    National Parks and Conservation Association
Barbara Pahl, Regional Director, Mountain/Plains Office, National Trust for Historic Preservation
Jim Quinn, Executive Director, Historic South Dakota Foundation, Inc.
Walt Roetter, Ellsworth Heritage Foundation

AIR FORCE

Sam Christian, US Air Force Museum
Dan Friese, Ellsworth AFB
Lt. Col. Dave Hockaday, Ellsworth AFB
Lt. Col. Tom Lillie, Headquarters, US Air Force
Col. Roscoe E. Moulthrop, US Strategic Command, Offutt AFB
Tim Pavek, Ellsworth AFB
Paul Williams, Headquarters, US Air Force

STATE OF SOUTH DAKOTA

Paul Putz, Director, Historic Preservation Center
Dee Dee Rapp, Department of Tourism

Left: *Test Launch of Minuteman I, Vandenberg Air Force Base.* US AIR FORCE

www.ingramcontent.com/pod-product-compliance
Lightning Source LLC
Chambersburg PA
CBHW080742250426
43671CB00038B/2838